THE ULTIMATE MAT GUIDE

UniAdmissions

Previous Editions: 2021, 2020, 2019

ISBN 978-1-915091-68-0

Published by *RAR Medical Services Limited*

www.uniadmissions.co.uk

info@uniadmissions.co.uk

+44 (0) 208 068 0438

ABOUT THE AUTHOR

Rohan is the **Director of Operations** at UniAdmissions and is responsible for its technical and commercial arms. He graduated from Gonville and Caius College, Cambridge and is a fully qualified doctor. Over the last five years, he has tutored hundreds of successful Oxbridge and Medical applicants. He has also authored ten books on admissions tests and interviews.

Rohan has taught physiology to undergraduates and interviewed medical school applicants for Cambridge. He has published research on bone physiology and writes education articles for the Independent and Huffington Post. In his spare time, Rohan enjoys playing the piano and table tennis.

THE ULTIMATE MAT GUIDE

ROHAN AGARWAL

UniAdmissions

THE BASICS

Congratulations on taking the first step to your MAT preparation! First used in 2007, the MAT is a difficult exam, and you'll need to prepare thoroughly in order to make sure you get that dream university place.

The *Ultimate MAT Guide* is the only MAT book currently available on the market, and the culmination of years of work from specialist MAT tutors at Uni Admissions.

While it might be tempting to dive straight in with mock papers, this is not a sound strategy. Firstly, start off by understanding the structure, syllabus, and theory behind the test. Once you're satisfied with this, move onto doing the past papers, which are all available for free on the Cambridge Assessment website. Start with the 2007 paper and work chronologically; and check your answers against the official solutions.

Once you're satisfied with this, complete your preparation with the 4 full-length practice exams found in *The Ultimate MAT Guide*.

As you've probably realised by now, there are well over a hundred questions to tackle, meaning that this isn't a test that you can prepare for in a single week. From our experience, the best students will prepare anywhere between four to eight weeks (although there are some notable exceptions!).

Remember that the route to a high score is your approach and practice. Don't fall into the trap that "you can't prepare for the MAT"– this could not be further from the truth. With knowledge of the test, some useful time-saving techniques and plenty of practice you can dramatically boost your score.

Work hard, never give up and do yourself justice. Good luck!

What is the MAT?

The Mathematics Admissions Test (MAT) is a two-hour written exam taken by prospective students applying for degrees in Mathematics and Computer Science at Oxford, Mathematics courses at Imperial College London, and Mathematics at the University of Warwick.

What does the MAT consist of?

Section	Timing	SKILLS TESTED	Questions	Calculator
ONE	150 Minutes	Maths AS level Some Maths A2 level topics	7 Questions: Answer 5, depending on the subject	Not Allowed

Why is the MAT used?

Maths applicants tend to be a bright bunch and therefore usually have excellent grades with many having over 90% in all of their A level subjects. This means that competition is fierce, and the universities must use the MAT to help differentiate between applicants. Oxford interview roughly 35% of their applicants - and a high MAT score is a great way to stand out throughout the entire application process, especially towards the end.

When do I sit MAT?

The MAT takes place in the first week of November every year, normally on a Wednesday morning. Though registration for the test must occur before a deadline in the middle of October.

Can I resit the MAT?

No, you can only sit the MAT once per admissions cycle.

Where do I sit the MAT?

You can usually sit the MAT at your school or college (ask your exams officer for more information). Alternatively, if your school isn't a registered test centre or you're not attending a school, you can sit the test at an external centre.

Do I have to resit the MAT if I reapply?

Yes - you cannot use your score from any previous attempts. This is to ensure that all applicants are being compared fairly, on the basis of their performance on the same exam on the same day.

How is the MAT Scored?

The paper unsurprisingly starts with question 1: this has 10 parts where each is a multiple-choice question (5 choices) - each carry with it 4 marks for a correct answer. Questions 2-7 are longer questions, usually with 3-5 parts, and are each in total worth 15 marks (see the 'Positive Marking' section for a breakdown). Each student will attempt up to 5 questions, the combinations of which are based on whether their application is to the Maths, Computer Science, or a joint honours course.

How is the MAT used?

Each university will place different weightings on different components so it's important you find out as much information about how your marks will be used by emailing the college admissions office. In general, the university will interview a high proportion of realistic applicants, so the MAT score isn't vital for making the interview shortlist. However, it can play a huge role in the final decision after your interview.

GENERAL ADVICE

Start Early

It is much easier to prepare if you practice little and often. Start your preparation well in advance, ideally by mid-September but at the latest by early October. This way you will have plenty of time to complete as many papers as you wish to feel comfortable and won't have to panic and cram just before the test, which is a much less effective and more stressful way to learn. In general, an early start will give you the opportunity to identify the complex issues and work at your own pace.

Prioritise

Some questions in the MAT can be long and complex – and given the intense time pressure, you need to know your limits. It is essential that you don't get stuck with very difficult questions. If part of a question looks particularly long or complex, mark it for review and move on. You don't want to be caught short at the end just because you got stuck on the final stage of a complicated question. If a question is taking too long, put it on to one side and move on. Take into account how the questions are weighted, so you can adjust your timing accordingly. Remember that question 1 is worth 40 marks, whilst questions 2-7 are only worth 15 marks. With practice and discipline, you can get very good at this and learn to maximise your efficiency.

Positive Marking

The first question in the paper is multiple choice and is made up of 10 different parts. There are no penalties for incorrect answers; you will gain four marks for each right answer and will not get any for each wrong or unanswered one. Your working is not marked in this question. This provides you with the luxury that you can always guess should you be unable to figure out the right answer for a question or run behind on time. Since each question provides you with 5 possible answers, you have a 20% chance of guessing correctly. Therefore, if you aren't sure (and are running short of time), then make an educated guess and move on. Before 'guessing' you should try to eliminate a couple of answers to increase your chances of getting the question correct. For example, if you manage to eliminate 2 options - your chances of getting the question increase from 20% to 33%! If you have failed to finish the exam, take the last 10 seconds to guess the remaining questions to at least give yourself a chance of getting them right.

Questions 2-7 are not multiple choice and working will be marked. Therefore, you need to write down all of your working to gain as many marks as possible. If your working and subsequently your answer is wrong, you will not lose any marks, but you will also not gain any. However, you may get credit for using the right methods or approach. If you are running out of time, it might be a good idea to outline the steps you would take if you had more time to let the examiner know that you haven't answered due to time pressure rather than due to lack of knowledge. Remember, it is better to NOT cross out working than to leave a question blank, it is hard for markers to award anything for crossed-out working. So, if in doubt: leave what you have written down and move on.

Practice

This is the best way of familiarising yourself with the style of questions and the timing for this section. Although the test is designed to be accessible based on your existing mathematical knowledge, you may not be familiar with the style of questions when you first encounter them. Therefore, you want to be comfortable at using this before you sit the test.

Practising questions will put you at ease and make you more comfortable with the exam. The more comfortable you are, the less you will panic on the test day and the more likely you are to score highly. Initially, work through the questions at your own pace, and spend time carefully reading the questions and looking at all the data provided. When it gets closer to the test, **make sure you practise the questions under exam conditions**.

Past Papers

The MAT is a well-established exam, and all the past papers are available online. Specimen papers are freely available online at www.uniadmissions.co.uk/MAT. Once you've worked your way through the questions in this book, you are highly advised to attempt them.

Keywords

Pay particular attention to the questions that contain key modifiers like "**always**", "**if**", "**if and only if**" as examiners like using them to make sure students know how to approach these questions. For example: "Is X always true?" elicits you to provide a counterexample to disprove the statement X, or a logical argument/proof to show that X is indeed always true (i.e. no counterexamples exist). "Does X hold if Y?" this requires a student to show that assuming Y is true *a priori*, does this lead to X? "Show that X holds if and only if Y" this requires the student to do TWO things, you need to prove both directions. First assuming X is true a priori, show it leads to Y; then secondly, assume Y is true a priori and show it leads to X".

The following classic example highlights the discrepancy between the statements: "The square of x is 4 if and only if x is 2" and "The square of x is 4 if x is 2". The first statement is false but the second is true, as the first makes a statement about uniqueness 'only if'. Let's work it through: (in the left direction) if x is 2, then it certainly is the case that the square is 4, (in the right direction) if x^2 is 4, then x is ±2, not just +2, so this doesn't hold, and the statement is false.

Calculators

Unfortunately for students, calculators are not allowed in the exam. This is because the examiners want to test your ability to solve problems, not to mindlessly bash away at a calculator. There are much better ways to challenge a student, and as they want to find the very best, they will use them. You can use this knowledge to your advantage – if you find yourself encountering a problem which seems impossible to tackle without a calculator, you've probably made a mistake.

Repeat Questions

When checking through answers, pay particular attention to questions you have got wrong. If there is a worked answer, look through that carefully until you feel confident that you understand the reasoning, and then repeat the question without help to check that you can do it. If only the answer is given, have another look at the question and try to work out why that answer is correct. This is the best way to learn from your mistakes and means you are less likely to make similar mistakes when it comes to the test.

The same applies for questions which you were unsure of and made an educated guess which was correct, even if you got it right. When working through this book, **make sure you highlight any questions you are unsure of**, this means you know to spend more time looking over them once marked.

Use the options for question 1:

In other cases, you may actually be able to use the options to arrive at the solution quicker than if you had tried to solve the question as you normally would. Consider the trivial example below:

A region is defined by the two inequalities: $x - y^2 > 1 \; and \; xy > 1$. Which of the following points is in the defined region?

A. (10,3)
B. (10,2)
C. (-10,3)
D. (-10,2)
E. (-10,-3)

Whilst it's possible to solve this question both algebraically or graphically by manipulating the identities, by far **the quickest way is to actually use the options**. Note that options C, D and E violate the second inequality, narrowing down to answer to either A or B. For A: 10 - 32 = 1 and thus this point is on the boundary of the defined region and not actually in the region. Thus, the answer is B (as 10-4 = 6 > 1).

It's worth noting, one can get caught up algebraically manipulating trigonometric identities and differentiating tedious expressions to find extrema of a function. Often looking at the options and reasoning based on observations such as cos(a) is between -1,1, so cos(a)2 is between 0,1 etc can make an intimidating question much easier to tackle. So definitely don't rule out using the options to guide you, especially if you are stuck.

A word on timing...

"If you had all day to do your MAT, you would get 100%. But you don't."

Whilst this isn't completely true, it illustrates a very important point. Once you've practised and know how to answer the questions, the clock is your biggest enemy. This seemingly obvious statement has one very important consequence. **The way to improve your MAT score is to improve your speed.** There is no magic bullet. But there are a great number of techniques that, with practice, will give you significant time gains, allowing you to answer more questions and score more marks.

Timing is tight throughout the MAT – **mastering timing is the first key to success**. Some candidates choose to work as quickly as possible to save up time at the end to check back, but this is generally not the best way to do it. MAT questions can have a lot of information in them – each time you start answering a question it takes time to get familiar with the instructions and information. By splitting the question into two sessions (the first run-through and the return-to-check) you double the amount of time you spend on familiarising yourself with the data, as you have to do it twice instead of only once. This costs valuable time.

In addition, candidates who do check back may spend 2–3 minutes doing so and yet not make any actual changes. Whilst this can be reassuring, it is a false reassurance as it is unlikely to have a significant effect on your actual score. Therefore, it is usually best to pace yourself very steadily and work very carefully to avoid making algebraic errors or unnecessary mistakes on your first attempt, and so removing the need to check back. Aim to split your time equally between questions (taking into account the different weightings of the questions) and to finish the last question just as time runs out. This reduces the time spent on re-familiarising with questions and maximises the time spent on the first attempt, gaining more marks.

It is essential that you don't get stuck with the hardest parts of a question – no doubt there will be some. In the time spent answering only one of these, you may miss out on answering three easier parts of another question. If a question is taking too long and you have done as much as you can, move on. Never see this as giving up or in any way failing, rather it is the smart way to approach a test with a tight time limit.

With practice and discipline, you can get very good at this and learn to maximise your efficiency. It is not about being a hero and aiming for full marks – this is almost impossible and very much unnecessary (even for Oxford!). It is about gaining the maximum possible number of marks within the time you have.

PRACTICE PAPERS

PRACTICE PAPER 1

I. For **ALL APPLICANTS**

A. The equation

$$4^{x-1} - 2^{x+1} = k$$

where k is a real number, obtains its minimum value when

A. $x = 0$
B. $x = 1$
C. $x = 2$
D. $x = -1$
E. $x = -\infty$

B. As x varies over the real numbers, the largest value taken by the function

$$(4\cos^2 x + 2\cos 4x + 3)^2$$

Equals

A. 81
B. $27 + 10\sqrt{2}$
C. 9
D. $39 + 12\sqrt{3}$
E. 49

C. Which of the following lines is tangent to the circle with the equation

$$(x-2)^2 + y^2 = 1?$$

A. $x + y = 3$
B. $y = x - \sqrt{2}$
C. $x + y = 2 - \sqrt{2}$
D. $x = 2 + \sqrt{2}$
E. $y = \frac{\sqrt{x}}{\sqrt{2}}$

D. A sequence (a_n) is defined by the relationship

$$a_{n+1} = \frac{a_n}{a_{n-1}}$$

for every $n \geq 2$ Given that $a_1 = 2$ and $a_2 = 8$, what is a_{2019}?

A. 8
B. $\frac{1}{8}$
C. $\frac{1}{4}$
D. 4
E. $\frac{1}{2}$

E. If the graph of $f(x)$ is given by

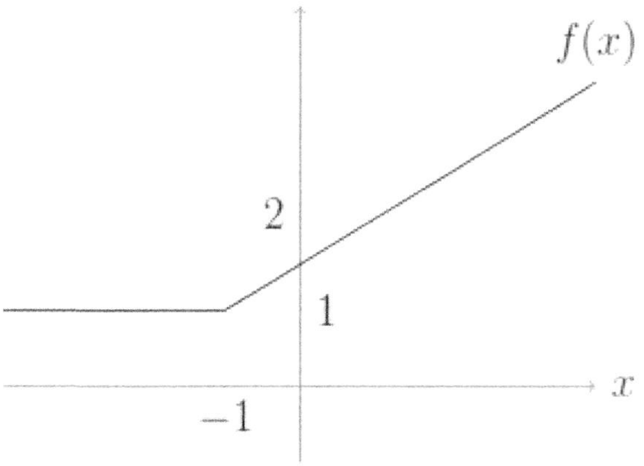

then the graph of $f(|x|-2)$ is given by

A

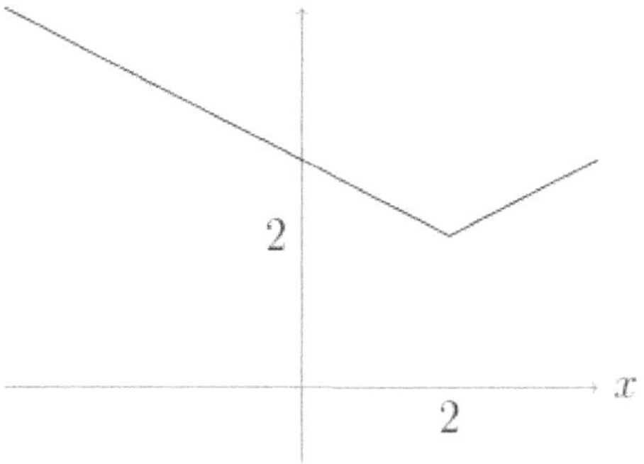

B

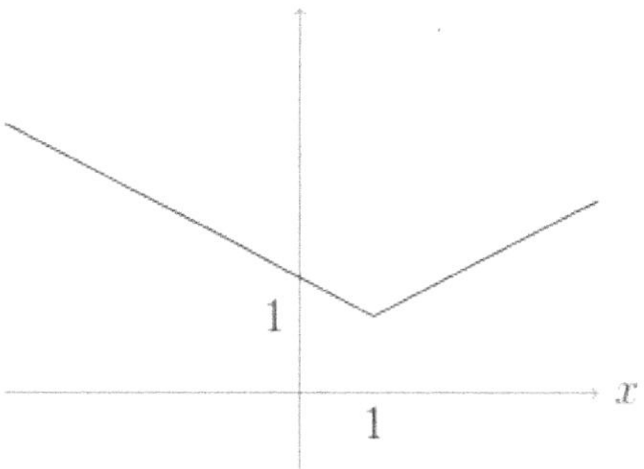

C

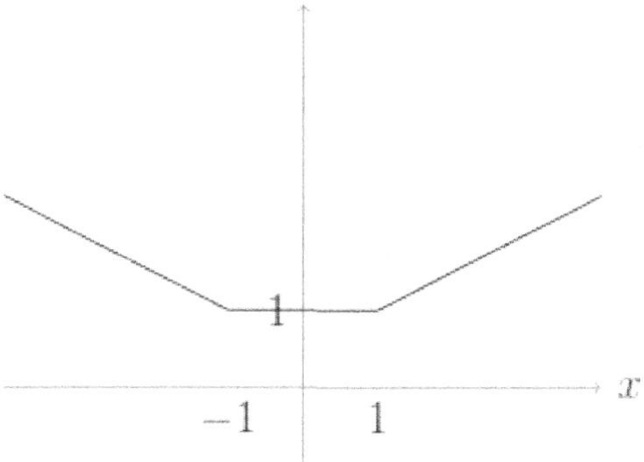

D

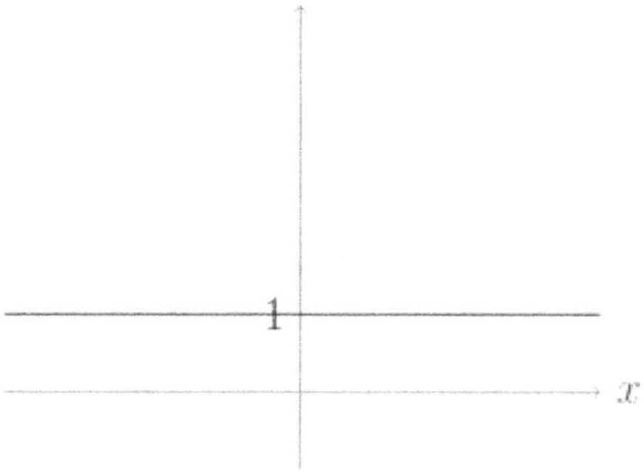

E

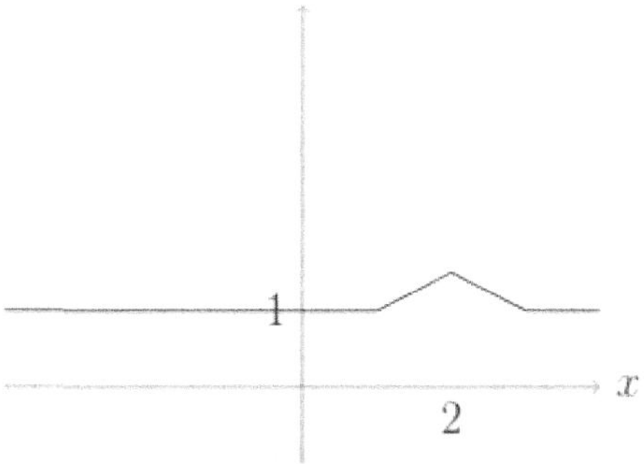

F. How many different *even* numbers of any length can be made from the digits

$$4, 7, 3, 8, 5$$

using each digit at most one time in each number?

A. 96 B. 130 C. 150 D. 64 E. 180

G. For what range of real values of k do the simultaneous equations

$$e^x - ke^y = 4$$

$$e^x + e^y = 2k$$

Have real solutions?

A. $k > -1$
B. $k > 2$ and $k < -1$,
C. $k > 2$
D. All values of k
E. No values of k

H. Consider a function $g(x)$ which is such that

$$g(\pi) = 2$$

$$g(0) = -1$$

What is the value of the integral

$$\int_0^\pi g(x)g'(x)\,dx?$$

A. $\frac{5}{2}$ B. 3 C. $\frac{3}{2}$ D. 1 E. $\frac{1}{2}$

I. Which figure shows the graph with equation

$$y = \frac{\sin^2 x}{x}?$$

A

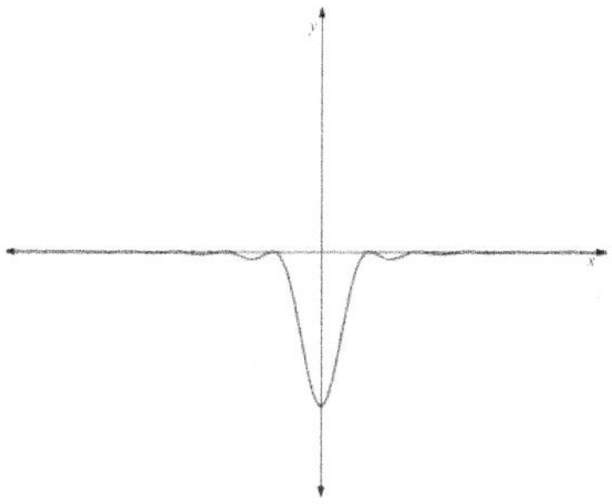

B

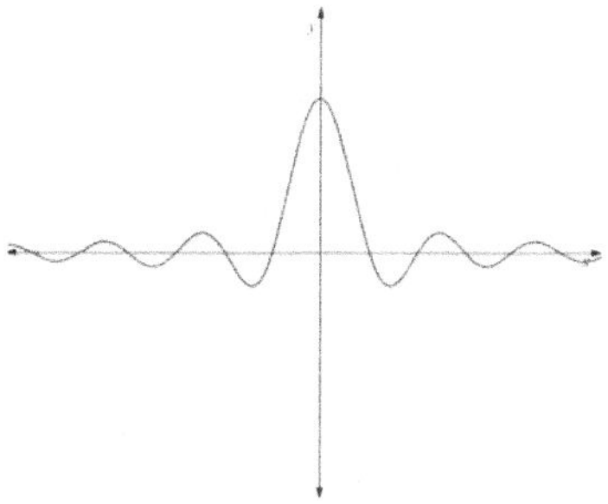

C

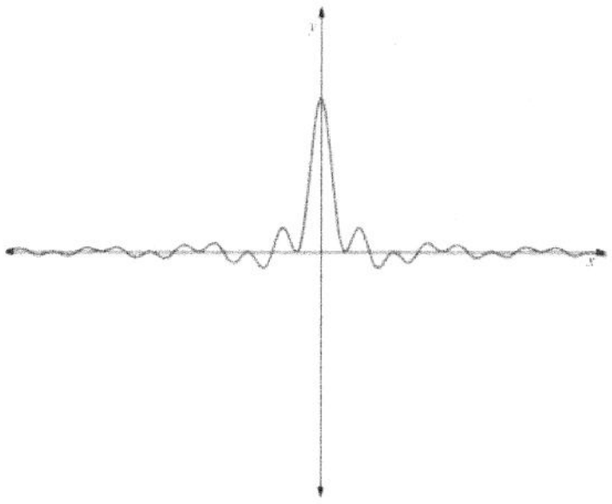

D

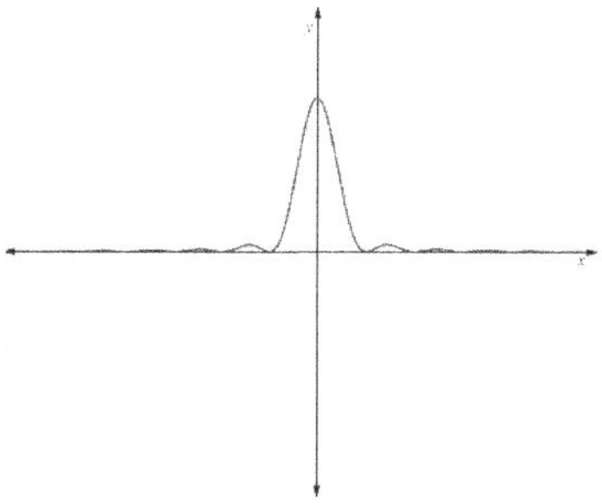

E

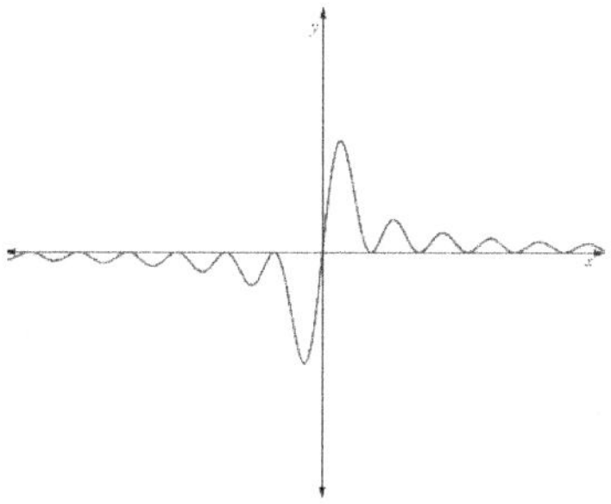

J. The diagram below shows a circle with a triangle XYZ inscribed. You are given that $XY = 15cm$, $YZ = 18cm$ and $XYZ = 60°$

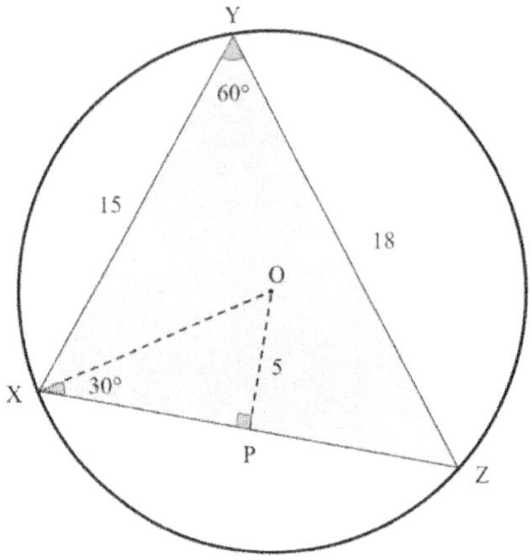

A right-angle triangle PXO is also shown. You are given that $OP = 5cm$ and $\hat{O}XP = 30°$

The shaded area is denoted by A_T with perimeter P_T, whilst the area of the circle is denoted by A_C with circumference P_C. Using the information provided, which of the following is true?

A. $P_T + P_C < A_T$
B. $2P_c > P_T$
C. $3A_T < A_C$
D. $2A_T + P_T > A_C$
E. Not enough information

2. For **ALL APPLICANTS**

Let a and b be real numbers. Consider the cubic

$$\eta = x^3 + bx^2 - ax - 2b + 1 \qquad (\dagger)$$

and the straight line given by

$$y = bx + a \qquad (\dagger\dagger)$$

(i) Show that the two curves always intersect at $x = -1$

(ii) Show that a necessary condition for three distinct points of intersection is

$$a > 3$$

(iii) For what values of a and b do the two curves only intersect at one point?

(iv) If $a = 3/4$, and the value of b for which $(\dagger)$ and $(\dagger\dagger)$ have the same gradient at precisely one point.

3. For **APPLICANTS IN**

- Mathematics
- Mathematics & Statistics
- Mathematics & Philosophy
- Mathematics & Computer Science

(i) On the axes below, sketch the graphs of $y = \sqrt{x}$ and $y = \frac{1}{2}x$

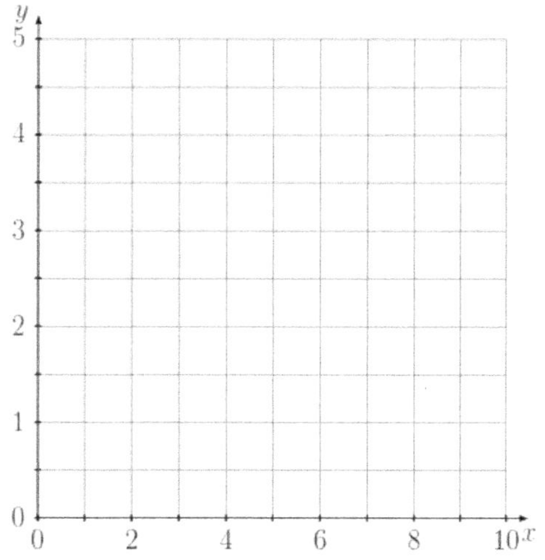

(ii) Find the coordinates of the two intersection points.

(iii) Find the area between the two curves

Now consider extending this idea by replacing the curve $y = \sqrt{x}$ with the general curve $y = \sqrt{kx}$ and the line $y = \frac{1}{2}x$ with the line $y = mx$, where $m, k \geq 0$.

(iv) Find a general result for the area $A(m;\ k)$ between the two curves.

(v) For what range of values of m and k is the enclosed area greater than the $x - coordinate$ of the non-zero point of intersection?

4. For **APPLICANTS IN**

- Mathematics
- Mathematics & Statistics
- Mathematics & Philosophy

Let Q denote the quarter-annulus of points $(x;\ y)$ such that $x \geq 0$, $y \geq 0$ and $1 \leq x^2 + y^2 \leq 4$ as drawn in Figures A and B below

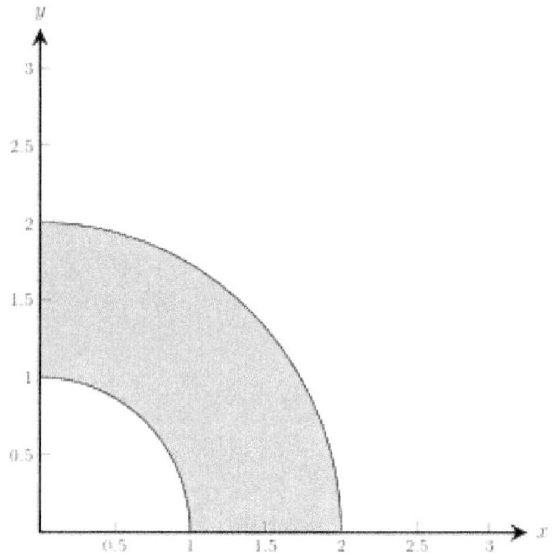

Figure A

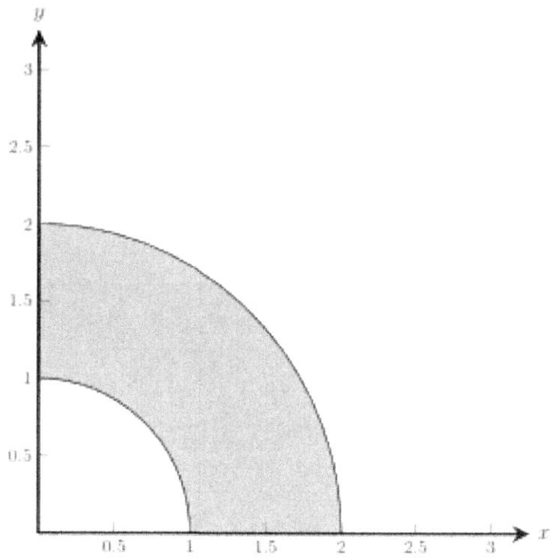

Figure B

(i) On the axes in Figure A, sketch the graphs of

$$x + y = \frac{3}{2}, \qquad x + y = 2, \quad x + y = 3.$$

What is the largest value of $x + y$ achieved at points $(x;\ y)$ in Q?

(ii) On the axes in Figure B, sketch the graphs of

$$xy = \frac{1}{2}, \quad xy = 1, \quad xy = 2.$$

What is the largest value of $x^2 + y^2 + 5xy$ achieved at points $(x;\ y)$ in Q?

What is the smallest value of $x^2 + y^2 - 4xy$ achieved at points $(x;\ y)$ in Q?

(iii) Describe the curve

$$x^2 + y^2 - 6x - 4y = k$$

where $k > -13$.

What is the largest value of $x^2 + y^2 - 6x - 4y$ achieved at points $(x;\ y)$ in Q?

5. For **ALL APPLICANTS**

A group of n soldiers are under siege and come up with a system to avoid getting captured alive by the enemy. They stand in a circle and the first soldier kills the soldier to the left of him. The next remaining living person to their left then kills the next living person to their left, and so on until one soldier remains.

(i) Which soldier survives when $n = 4$? What about when $n = 8$?

We observe that the same soldier appears to survive when n is of the form 2^k and wish to prove that this holds for $k > 3$.

(ii) By considering relabelling the surviving soldiers after the one lap of the circle, or otherwise, show that our hypothesis holding for 2^k proves that it also holds for 2^{k+1}.

We can uniquely write any positive integer in terms of a largest possible power of 2 and some remainder, i.e., as $2^a + r$ For example, the number 72 can be written as $2^6 + 8$.

(iii) With this in mind, derive a formula for the surviving soldier in terms of a and r in the general case $n = 2^a + r$.

Hint: Think about how many steps it takes for there to be 2^a *soldiers remaining.*

A **Mersenne prime** is any prime number that can be written in the form $2^k - 1$.

(iv) Using your formula from part (iii), deduce which soldier survives when n is a Mersenne prime.

6. For **APPLICANTS IN**

- Computer Science
- Mathematics & Computer Science
- Computer Science & Philosophy

An island is inhabited solely by knights who always tell the truth and knaves who always lie.
Archie and Bertie are residents of the island.
Archie says, "We are both knaves".

(i) What are Archie and Bertie?

David, Edgar and Felix are three other inhabitants of the island.

David says "I am a knight" or "I am a knave" - we don't yet know which. Edgar then says "David said "I am a knight" and "Felix is a knave". Finally, Felix says "David is a knight".

(ii) What are David, Edgar and Felix?

A random sample of $2n$ islanders then form a circle. One by one, each says "the person on my right is a knave".

(iii) What is the largest possible number of knights in the circle?

(iv) What about if the circle was increased to $2n + 1$ inhabitants?

One of the knights on the island then goes rogue and becomes a spy. Spies can either tell the truth or lie. The rest of the knights know who the spy is.

(v) In a group of 100 people containing 99 knights and 1 spy, suggest a strategy for identifying the spy in as few questions as possible.

(vi) Is it possible to identify the spies in a group containing 51 spies and 49 knights? Explain your answer.

7. For **APPLICANTS IN**

- Computer Science
- Computer Science & Philosophy

Passwords are sequences of the letters a and b. The *length* of a password is the number of letters in the sequence.

(i) Write down all possible passwords of length 3.

(ii) How many unique possible passwords of length n are there?

Now suppose that the letter b cannot occur twice in a row, i.e. bab is allowed but bba is not. Let C_n represent the number of passwords of length n that satisfy this rule.

(iii) What are C_2 and C_3?

(iv) Show that for $n \geq 4$ we have the recurrence relation

$$C_n = C_{n-1} + C_{n-2}$$

Hint: separate the case where the last letter is b from the case where it is a.

Finally, suppose that we also cannot have passwords which start and end with the letter b. Let P_n be the number of passwords satisfying this property.

(v) For $n \geq 5$, write down a formula for P_n in terms of C_i and justify your answer

PRACTICE PAPER 2

1. For **ALL APPLICANTS**

A. What is the total area of the region bounded by the x axis, the lines $x = 1$ and $x = 3$ and the curve $y = x^3 - 6x^2 + 11x - 6$?

A. $\frac{9}{4}$ B. $\frac{1}{2}$ C. $\frac{1}{4}$ D. $\frac{2}{3}$ E. 0

B. What is the maximum value of the following function?

$$f(x) = \ln(-4x^2 + 12x - 8)$$

A. -8 B. $\frac{1}{2}$ C. -4 D. 0 E. 1

C. How many negative roots does the following function have?

$$f(x) = 15x^4 + 32x^3 + 24x^2 + 8x + 1$$

A. 0 B. 1 C. 2 D. 3 E. 4

D. The function $y = kx + 1$ satisfies

$$\frac{d^2y}{dx^2} + \left(\frac{dy}{dx}\right)^2 + \frac{dy}{dx} = 1$$

for which of the following statements?

A. No values of k
B. Exactly one value of k
C. Exactly two distinct values of k
D. Exactly three distinct values of k
E. Infinitely many values of k

E. A sequence (a_n) has first term $a_1 = 1$ and the recurrence relation $a_{n+1} = a_n + n - 1$. What is a_{100}?

A. 4951
B. 5589
C. 4852
D. 4124
E. 5013

F. How many solutions does the following equation have in the range $-\frac{\pi}{2} \leq x \leq \frac{\pi}{2}$?

$$4\sin^2(x)\cos(x) - 8\sin^2(x) - 9\cos(x) + 9 = 0$$

A. 0 B. 1 C. 2 D. 3 E. 4

G. Which of the following is the graph of $\eta = (x-2)^2 \sin(\pi x)$?

A

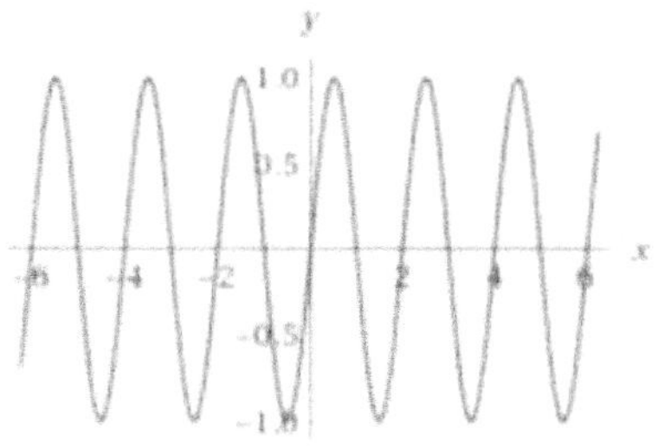

B

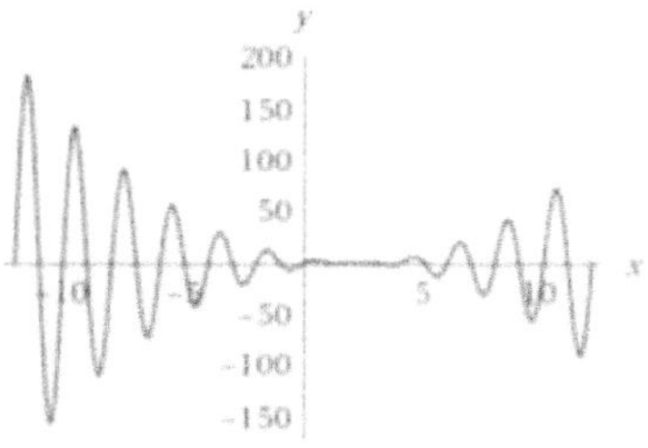

C

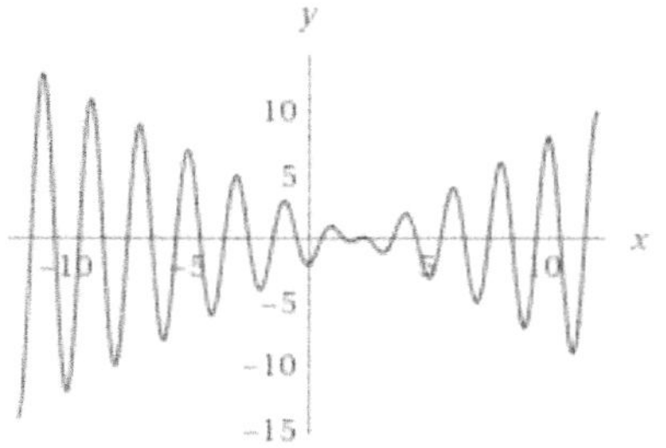

D

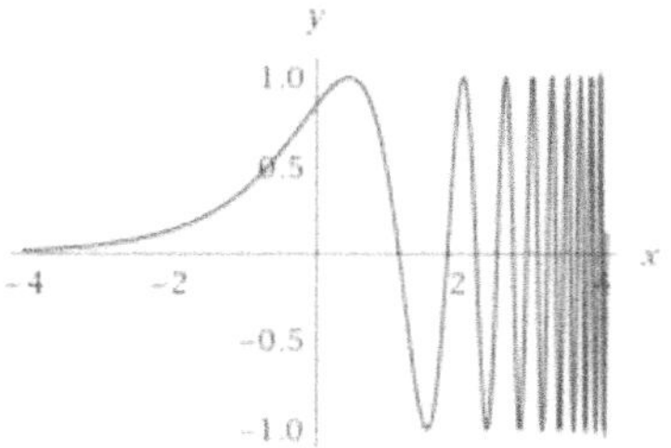

E

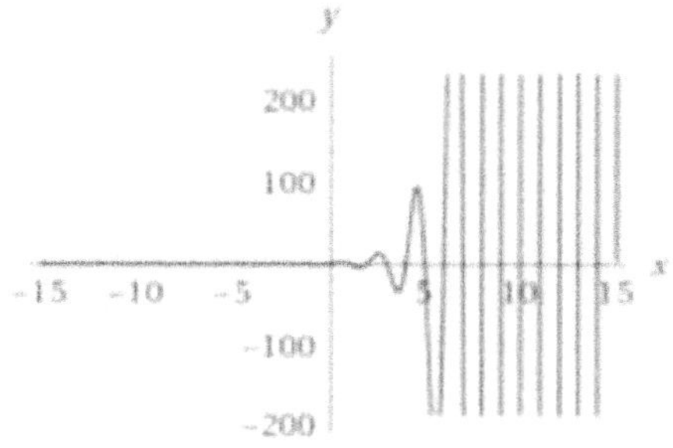

H. How many solutions does the following equation have?

$$e^{4x} - 8e^{3x} + 24e^{2x} - 32e^{x} + 15 = 0$$

A. 0 B. 1 C. 2 D. 3 E. 4

I. A function $f(x)$ has properties $f(1) = 1$ and $f(2x+1) = -f(x)$ for all positive integers x. What is the value of $f(2^6 - 1) + f(2^7 - 1)$?

A. -2 B. -1 C. 0 D. 1 E. 2

J. A square is inscribed in a circle of radius $\sqrt{2}$. An isosceles triangle is inscribed in the square. What is the area of the shaded region?

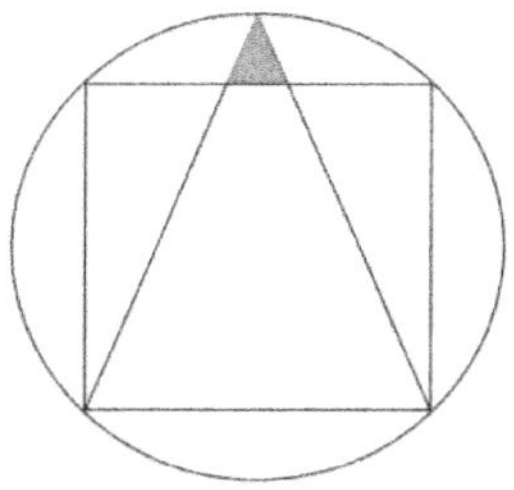

A $5\sqrt{2} - 7$

B $\frac{1}{3}$

C $4\sqrt{2}$

D $\frac{1}{10}$

E $\sqrt{2} - 1$

2. For **ALL APPLICANTS**

The sequence (x_n) is defined by $x_1 = 1$ and $x_{n+1} = 1 + \frac{1}{x_n}$

(i) Evaluate $x_1 x_2 x_3 x_4 x_5$

(ii) There exists a sequence (u_n) such that $(x_n) = \frac{u_{n+1}}{u_n}$ for all positive integers n. Find a recurrence relation for (u_n) i.e., find constants a_k such that

$$u_n = \sum_{k=1}^{\mathrm{n}-1} a_k u_k$$

(iii) Suppose that $u_n = p^n$ for some p. Find all possible values of p.

(iv) Let p_1 and p_2 be the possible values of p. Find constants c_1 and c_2 such that

$$u_n = c_1 p_1^n + c_2 p_2^n$$

And show that this formula folds for all n.

(v) Hence find an expression for $x_1 x_2 x_3 \dots x_n$.

3. Only for **APPLICANTS IN:**

- Mathematics
- Mathematics & Statistics
- Mathematics & Philosophy
- Mathematics & Computer Science

For each strictly positive integer k, let $f_k(x) = 1 + x + \cdots + x^k$ for $-1 \le x \le 1$.

(i) On the same axes, sketch $f_k(x)$ for $k = 1,2,3,4,5,6$.
Hint: consider $f_{k+2}(x) - f_k(x)$.

(ii) Find an expression for $a(k)$, defined as the area of the region enclosed between the lines $y = f_{k+2}(x)$ and $y = f_k(x)$

(iii) Let

$$A(n) = \sum_{k=1}^{n} a(k)$$

Describe the behaviour of $A(n)$ as n becomes large.

(iv) Hence find the area of the region between

$$y = 1 + x + x^2$$
$$y = 1 + x$$
$$x = -1$$

4. Only for **APPLICANTS IN:**

- Mathematics
- Mathematics & Statistics
- Mathematics & Philosophy

The diagram shows two lines in the plane, intersecting at a point Q. The line joining O and Q creates an angle θ with the x axis, while the line joining P, Q and R creates an angle α with the x axis, as shown in the diagram. Point P is located at $(1, 0)$.

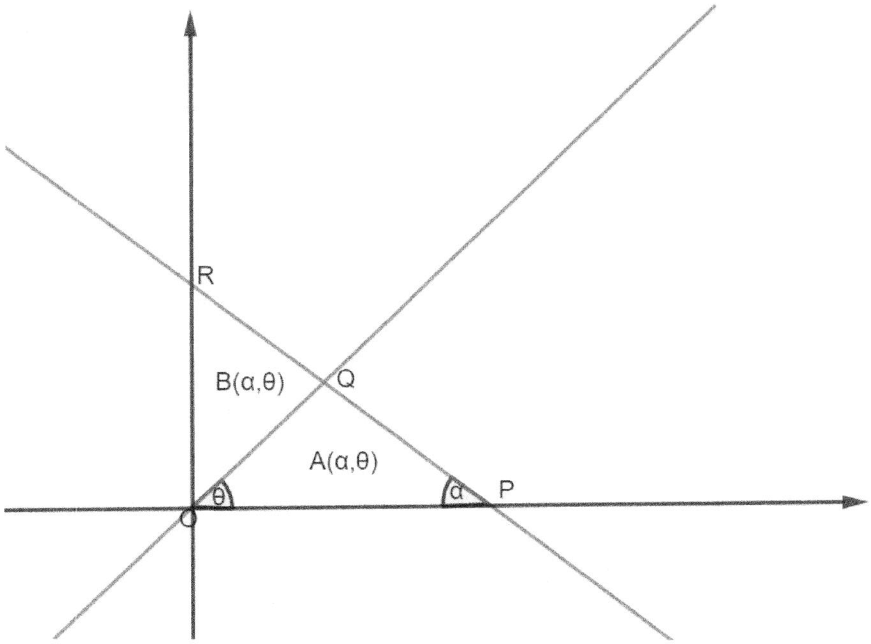

Figure 1: Not to scale

(i) Find, in terms of α, the equation of the line joining points P, Q and R.

(ii) Find, in terms of θ, the equation of the line joining O and R. Hence write, in terms of α and θ, the coordinates of point Q.

Triangle OPQ has area $A(\alpha, \theta)$ and triangle OQR has area $B(\alpha, \theta)$.

(iii) Give an example of an α and θ such that $A(\alpha, \theta) = B(\alpha, \theta)$. In addition, show that when $A(\alpha, \theta) = B(\alpha, \theta), A(\alpha, \theta)$ is independent of θ.

(iv) Find an expression for $A(\alpha, \theta)$ in terms of α and θ.

(v) Now let $\alpha = \frac{\pi}{4}$. Find the value of $tan(\theta)$ such that $A(\frac{\pi}{4}, \theta) = \frac{1}{2} B(\frac{\pi}{4}, \theta)$.

5. For **ALL APPLICANTS**

Consider n children standing in a circle playing a game where they are throwing a ball to a person on their left. They wish to design a game where each child throws the ball to the xth person on their left but no child is left out of the game $(1 \leq x \leq n)$.

(i) What are the possible values of x when $n = 3,4,5,6$?

(ii) For a general n describe the possible values of x.

(iii) If n is a prime, how many possible values of x are there? Justify your answer.

(iv) Suppose all of the local schools play this game together. There are 5040 children. What is the smallest possible value of x?

6. Only for **APPLICANTS IN:**

- Computer Science
- Mathematics & Computer Science
- Computer Science & Philosophy

Some people are dealt cards which tell them exactly how to act. They say either: "You must always tell the truth" or "You must lie exactly once". Each person can see everyone else's cards.

(i) Suppose that there are two people and one of each type of card. First, person A says: "person B has the liar card". And person B says: "person A has the liar card". Then, A says: "Today is Monday", and B says: "I have the truth card". Who has the liar card?

For the rest of the question assume that there are more than one of each card (so A and B can have the same type of card).

(ii) Does the above conversation contain enough information to know which cards A and B have? Explain your answer and give any conclusions that can be made.

(iii) Suppose a new person C says first: "B has a liar card" and then "I have a truth card". Does this change the conclusions you can make?

(iv) A new person D enters the room. And players A-D are re-dealt cards.

Person A says: "I have a truth card" and "It is sunny".

Person B says "It is after 2 pm" and "Exactly one of us has a truth card". Person C says "It is not sunny" and "Person A has a truth card".

Person D says "5 is less than 3" and "It is before 2 pm".

Who has the truth card?

7. Only for **APPLICANTS IN:**

- Computer Science
- Computer Science & Philosophy

A game consists of two players attempting to get their counter to the other side of a board before their opponent. The game is played on a board with each side being made up of an odd number of squares. Each player has a counter which starts on the middle square of opposing edges. The players take alternating turns moving their counter to an adjacent (left/right/up/down) unoccupied square - so the players can "block" each other.

Consider a 3x3 board. Assume Player A moves first.

(i) How many different possibilities are there for their first two moves (Player A's first move followed by Player B's first move)?

(ii) Does the number of possible second moves for A depend on B's first move? Justify your answer.

(iii) Hence calculate the number of possibilities for the first three moves.

(iv) Can either player win within the first 3 (total) moves? Explain your answer. Suppose extra points are awarded for winning within the first 3 moves.

(v) What should A's first move be?

(vi) Given that A makes the best possible first move, can B win?

Suppose A makes the same opening move, but the game is now played on a board with sides of length 2n $(n > 1)$, and the counters start in the top and bottom left corners

PRACTICE PAPER 3

1. For **ALL APPLICANTS**

A. The sum

$$\sum_{k=0}^{\infty} \frac{3^{k+1} - 2^k}{6^k}$$

is equal to

A. $\frac{1}{2}$ B. 2 C. $\frac{3}{2}$ D. $\frac{9}{2}$ E. 4

B. How many distinct real solutions does the following equation have?

$$\log_{x^2+1}(3x^2 + 7) = 2$$

A. None B. 1 C. 2 D. 3 E. 4

C. What is the $x - coordinate$ of the point on the curve

$$x^2 - 6x + y^2 - 4y + 9 = 0$$

nearest the origin?

A. $2 - \frac{4}{13}\sqrt{13}$
B. $2 - \sqrt{13}$
C. 2
D. 1
E. $3 - \frac{6}{13}\sqrt{13}$

D. What is the smallest positive root of the following trigonometric equation?

$$\sqrt{2} \sin x = 2 \cos \frac{1}{2} x$$

A. $x = 0$
B. $x = \frac{\pi}{2}$
C. $x = \frac{\pi}{4}$
D. $x = \frac{\pi}{3}$
E. $x = \frac{\pi}{8}$

E. A rectangle is inscribed inside an equilateral triangle, as shown in the diagram below.

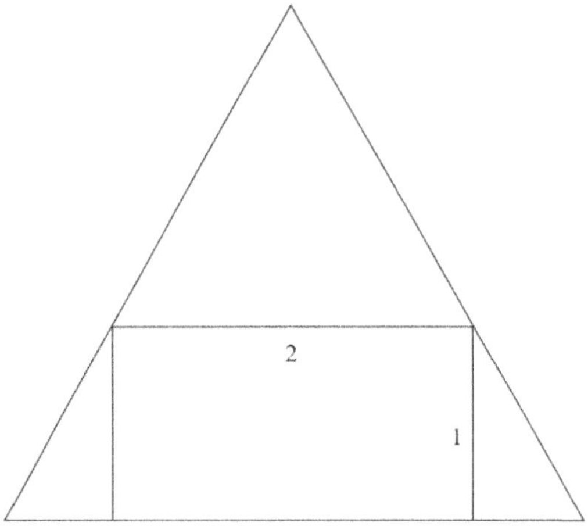

Not to Scale

What is the perimeter of the triangle?

A. 12
B. $6 + 3\sqrt{2}$
C. $6 + 2\sqrt{3}$
D. $12 - 3\sqrt{2}$
E. Need more information

F. Let n be an integer and define the functions $f(x)$ and $g(x)$ by

$$f(x) = x^2$$

$$g(x) = (x+4)^n - (x+1)^n(x+1)^{n^2}$$

Then $x^2 + 3$ is a factor of $g(f(x))$ for

A. Even n
B. $n = 0$ only
C. Odd n
D. $n = 0$
E. $n = -1$ only

G. Which function could be shown in the sketch below?

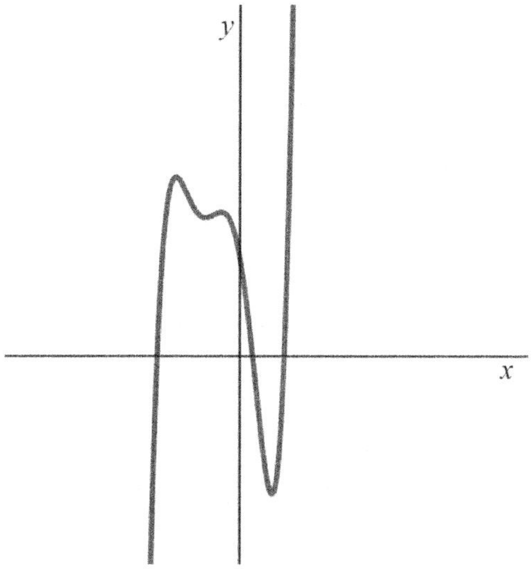

A. $y = x^5 + 6x^4 + 4x^2 + 3x - 1$
B. $y = x^5 + 3x^4 - 6x^2 - 5x + 3$
C. $y = x^5 - x^4 - 2x^3 + 2x^2 + x + 3$
D. $y = x^9 - x^4 + x^2 - 3x + 3$
E. $y = x^5 - 2x^4 - 2x^3 + 2x^2 + 4$

H. For what values of a and b are all stationary points of the curve

$$y = -x^4 + 2bx^3 + 6ax^2 - x + 3$$

maxima?

A. $b^2 < -4a$
B. $b^2 = 4a$
C. $b^2 > -4a$
D. $b = -3a$
E. All a and b

I. Consider the integral

$$\mathrm{I} = \int_0^{0.5} \ln(2x^2 - x + 1) \cdot \sin(k\pi x) \cdot \cos(k\pi x)\, dx$$

Where $k \geq 0$ is an integer. For which values of k does $\mathrm{I} = 0$?

A. $k = 0$
B. $k \geq 2$
C. $k \neq 1$
D. All even
E. All odd

J. Consider the sequence defined by the recurrence relation

$$u_{n+1} = 2u_n + 3$$
$$u_0 = 1$$

For what value of k is the following statement first true?

$$\sum_{n=0}^{k} u_n \geq 2^{12}$$

A. $k = 17$
B. $k = 8$
C. $k = 9$
D. $k = 10$
E. $k = 11$

2. For **ALL APPLICANTS**

A mathematician hints that in n^3 years, their age will be a perfect cube.

(i) By factorising, write the mathematician's current age as the product of two integers.

(ii) Show that in order for the mathematician's current age to be prime, the mathematician must be $3n^2 + 3n + 1$ years old.

The mathematician now reveals that in n^3 years their age will be both a perfect cube and a perfect square.

(iii) Show that all numbers which are both perfect cubes and perfect squares can be written as the sixth power of a positive integer.

Hint: consider writing the square and the cube in terms of their prime factors.

(iv) Using your answer to (ii), show that by summing over n we can derive the following formula for the sum of the squares of the first k positive integers

$$\sum_{n=1}^{k} n^2 = \frac{k(k+1)(2k+1)}{6}$$

3. For **APPLICANTS IN**

- Mathematics
- Mathematics & Statistics
- Mathematics & Philosophy
- Mathematics & Computer Science

A function, f, has two properties:

1. $f(x+y) = f(x) + f(y)$
2. $f(ax) = af(x)$

where a is a *positive* real number.

(i) Using both of the above properties, show that the function is *antisymmetric*, i.e. $f(-x) = -f(x)$

The ceiling function returns the next integer greater than or equal to its input. For example, the ceiling of π is 4.

(ii) Does the ceiling function satisfy the properties of f? Justify your answer.

We wish to use the properties of f to simplify the result of the trapezium rule when estimating the integral

$$\int_0^{10} f(x)\,dx \qquad \dagger$$

(iii) Using 10 trapezia, find an approximation for $(\dagger)$ in terms of $f(1)$.

(iv) Using an arbitrary number of trapezia, find an approximation and hence write down the exact value of $(\dagger)$ in terms of $f(1)$.

(v) What is the value of

$$\int_{-10}^{-5} f(x)\,dx$$

in terms of $f(1)$?

4. For **APPLICANTS IN**

- Mathematics
- Mathematics & Statistics
- Mathematics & Philosophy

Figure 1 shows a circle containing a triangle formed by connecting opposite ends of the diameter at a point on the circle's circumference. The triangle is then divided into two other triangles at a point O on the diameter. Important sides and angles are labelled.

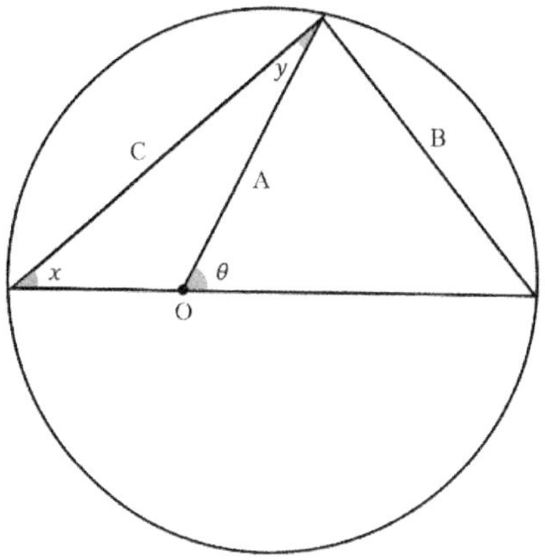

Figure 1: Not to scale

(i) Show that $\theta = x + y$

(ii) Using the sine rule, or otherwise, show that

$$\cos(x) = \frac{A}{B}\sin(x + y)$$

(iii) Using (ii), show further that

$$\sin^2(x + y) = \frac{B^2C^2}{A^2(B^2 + C^2)}$$

(iv) Find a necessary condition in terms of $tan(y)$ for the two smaller triangles to have equal area.

Finally, you are now given that $B = 6$ and $C = 8$.

(v) How far along the diameter should point O be in order for the triangles to have the same area?

Hint: You may find it useful to consider applying the cosine rule.

5. For **ALL APPLICANTS**

The Fibonacci sequence is defined by the recurrence relation

$$F_n = F_{n-1} + F_{n-2}$$

$$F_0 = 0 \qquad F_1 = 1$$

In other words, the previous two terms are added to give the next term in the sequence.

(i) Write down the first 5 terms in the sequence

We can write the nth term of the Fibonacci sequence in the form

$$F_n = A\lambda_+^n + B\lambda_-^n$$

where $\lambda_\pm$ are the roots of some polynomial and A and B are scalar coefficients.

(ii) By substituting $F_n = \lambda^n$ into the recurrence relation and solving the resulting quadratic, find the values of λ_+ and λ_-.

(iii) Substitute in the first two terms in the sequence to show that

$$F_n = \frac{1}{\sqrt{5}}\left[\left(\frac{1+\sqrt{5}}{2}\right)^n - \left(\frac{1-\sqrt{5}}{2}\right)^n\right]$$

(iv) Using your answer, find an expression for the sum of the first $k+1$ terms of the Fibonacci sequence (i.e. $F_0 + F_1 + \ldots + F_k$).

We can adapt the Fibonacci sequence by changing the value of the first terms. Consider an adapted sequence G_n which is the same as the Fibonacci sequence but has initial terms $G_0 = 1$ and $G_1 = 3$.

(v) Find an expression for G_n that is valid for $n > 1$.

(vi) Using your answer to (v), find a formula for the sum of the first $k+1$ terms in the sequence G_n.

6. For **APPLICANTS IN**

- Computer Science
- Mathematics & Computer Science
- Computer Science & Philosophy

A small village with n houses has strict requirements for a new plumbing system. Water must be piped from the reservoir to each house via some network of pipes. Water cannot flow back along a pipe it just came from and must only return to the reservoir once all houses have been visited at least once.

For example, when $n = 3$ a permissible structure of the plumbing network would be

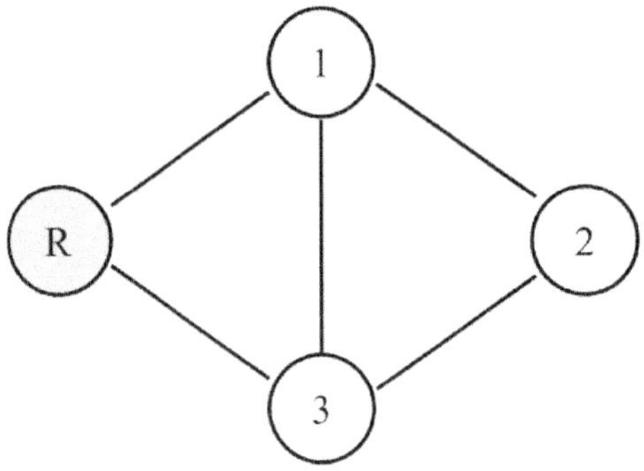

(i) Draw a permissible structure for the plumbing network when $n = 4$.

(ii) What is the minimum number of pipes needed for a plumbing network of size n? Justify your answer.

The local water board brings in a new regulation which states that the network still has to be permissible if one of the houses and all adjoining water pipes are removed.

(iii) Adapt your answer from (i) to meet this new regulation.

(iv) What is the minimum number of pipes now needed for a plumbing network of size n? Justify your answer.

Hint: separate the case where n is even from the case where n is odd.

Finally, a house's *water quality* is determined by the number of pipes connected to it. For instance, in our example house 3 has water quality of 3 whilst house 2 has water quality of 2.

(v) In a town of n people meeting the water board regulations with the minimum possible number of pipes, is it true that the sum of every house's water quality is always a multiple of 3? Justify your answer.

7. For **APPLICANTS IN**

- Computer Science
- Computer Science & Philosophy

MW-words are formed using the letters M and W. The inverse of a word is defined by flipping every letter so that every M becomes a W, and vice-versa. For example, the inverse of the word $MWMM$ is $WMWW$. We denote the inverse operator by the superscript x^{-1}.

MW-words are all generated according to one rule, starting with the word M:

1. If x is a word then xx^{-1} is a word

(i) Write down all MW words up to length 8

(ii) Show that all MW words of length 2^{2n} are *palindromic* (that is to say, they read the same back-to-front).

We now introduce a new operator - a rotation by 180 degrees, denoted by x^*. For example, the word $MWMM$ would become $WWMW$.

From this, we introduce a second rule:

2. If x is a word then x^* is a word.

(iii) Show that words of length 2^{2n+1} are unchanged by the rotation operator.

(iv) What happens to words of length 2^{2n} under the rotation operator?

(v) Using these two rules, why can we never have the same letter appearing 3 times in a row? Propose a third rule which would enable this.

PRACTICE PAPER 4

1. For **ALL APPLICANTS**

A. Let r and s be integers.

$$\frac{15^{r+s} \times 9^{r+s} \times 2^{r+3s}}{6^{2r+s} \times 5^{s} \times 3^{4s}}$$

is an integer if

A. $r \leq 2s$
B. $r = 2s$ and $r \geq 0$
C. $r \geq 0$
D. $r \geq 2s$
E. $r \geq 3s \geq 0$

B. Suppose that the function $y = f(x)$ has a local minimum at $(x_1, f(x_1))$. Then the function

$$y = a + bf(x + c)$$

has a local maximum at $(0, 0)$ when

A. $a = f(x_1)$, $b = 1$, $c = \frac{1}{x_1}$
B. $a = x_1$, $b = -f(x_1)$, $c = 1$
C. $a = -f(x_1)$, $b = -x_1$, $c = -1$
D. $a = f(x_1)$, $b = -1$, $c = x_1$
E. $a = -f(x_1)$, $b = x_1$, $c = 1$

C. If the polynomial

$$x^3 + ax^2 + bx + c$$

has three consecutive integer roots then

A. $b = \frac{3c}{a} + \frac{4a^2}{9}$
B. $b = a + c$
C. $b = a^2 + ac + c^2$
D. $b = ac$
E. $b = \frac{3a}{c} + \frac{4c^2}{9}$

D. In which of the marked, equal regions of the unit circle does $sin(2x) \geq sin\ x$ hold?

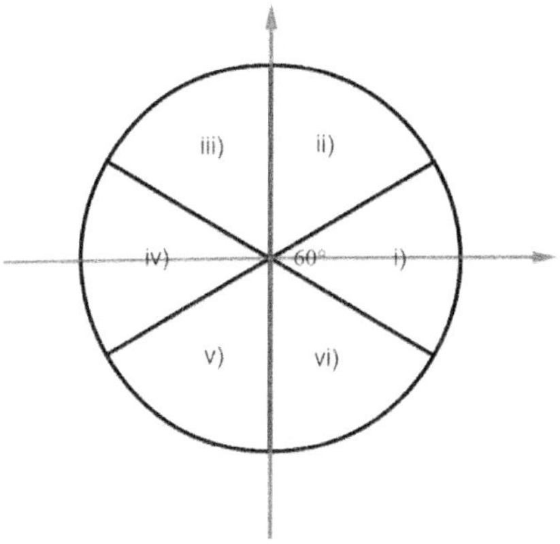

Not to scale

A. i and vi
B. ii, iii and vi
C. ii and iv
D. i, iv and v
E. i and iv

E. Which of the following is the graph of $y = \log(x \sin(x^2))$

A

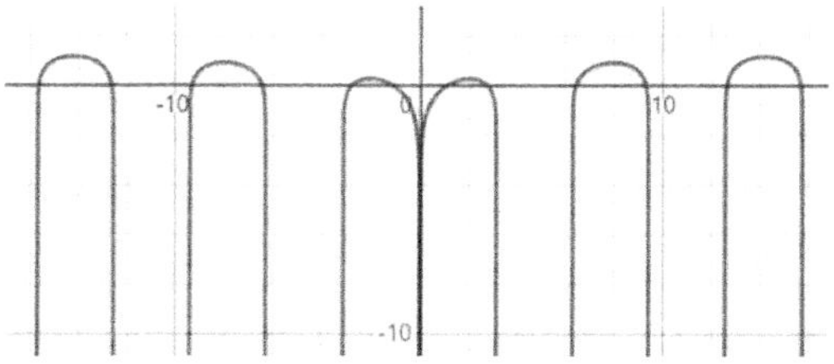

B

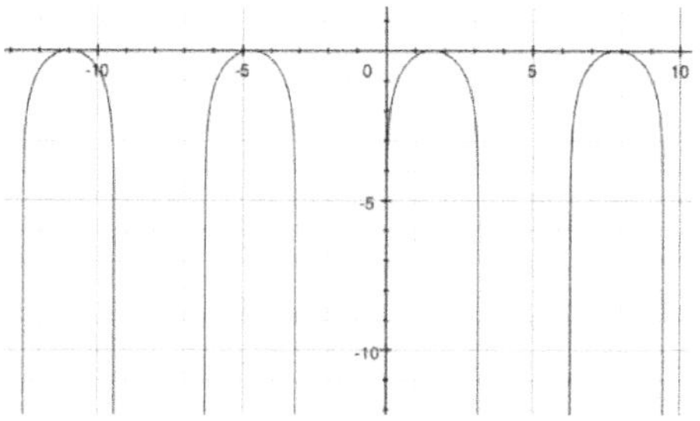

C

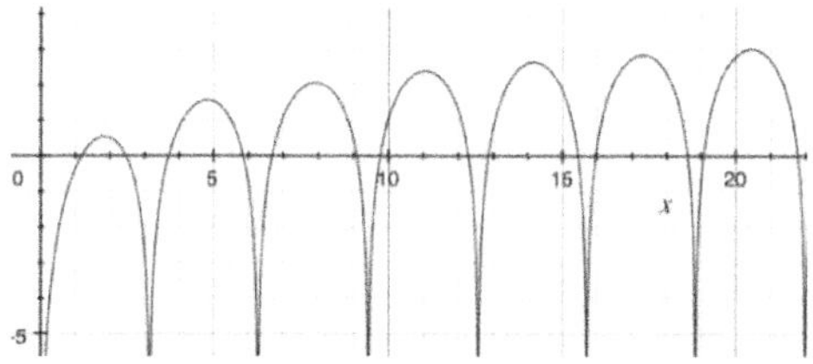

D

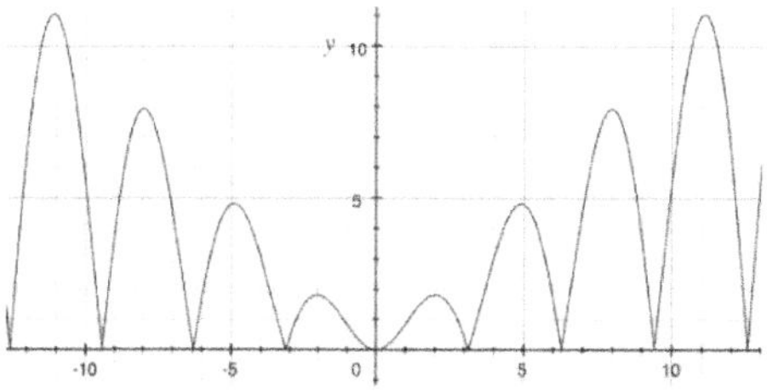

E

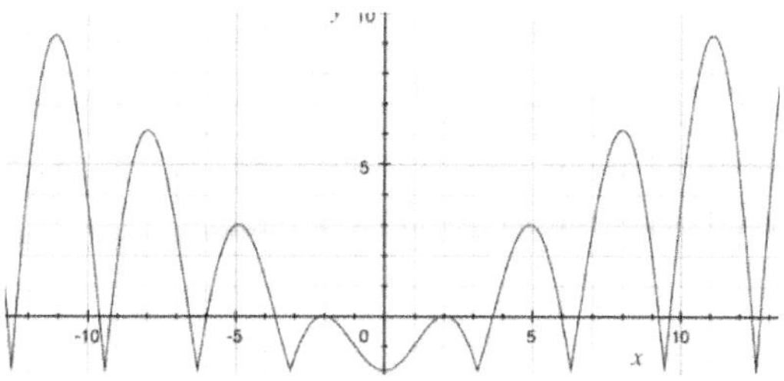

F. For which values of A in the range $0 \leq A < 2\pi$ does

$$\frac{1}{x} - x = 2\tan A$$

have at least one solution?

A. $0 < A < \pi$
B. $0 \leq A \leq \frac{\pi}{2}$
C. $\pi < A < 2\pi$
D. $0 \leq A \leq \frac{\pi}{3}$
E. all values of A

G. To be awarded a £100n prize, students must score at least 50% on n different exams, where n is a positive integer. Suppose that 6 students are taking these exams, and for every exam, every result is equally likely. Furthermore, individual exam results are independent. What is the probability that 2 of these 6 students received a £100n prize?

A. $\frac{15(2^n-1)^4}{2^{6n}}$
B. 2^{-2n}
C. $\frac{(2^n-1)^4}{2^{2n}}$
D. $\frac{(2^n-1)^2}{2^{2n}}$
E. $\frac{6(2^n-1)^4}{2^{6n}}$

H. What is the maximum possible value of the following equation?

$$y = \frac{1}{\cos(x) + 2} - \frac{1}{\cos(x) + 3}$$

A. $\frac{3}{4}$
B. $\frac{1}{2}$
C. -4
D. $\frac{1}{6}$
E. 1

I. Suppose that a function $f(x)$ has the following properties:

$$f(-x) = -f(x)$$
$$f(x) = f(4 - x)$$
$$\frac{1}{f(x)} = 0 \ at \ x = 0$$

Which of the following must be a section of the graph $y = f(x)$?

A

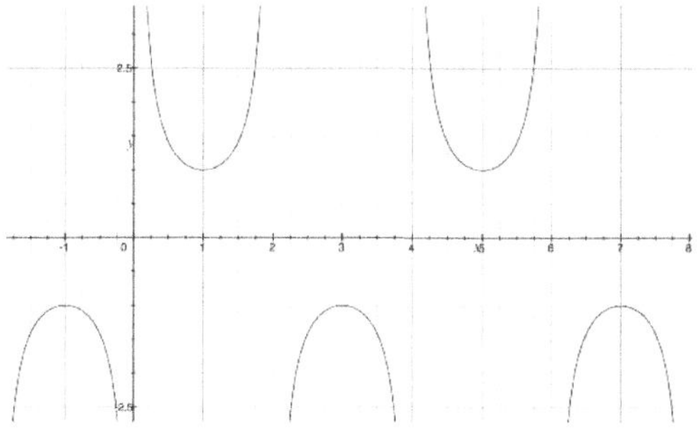

B

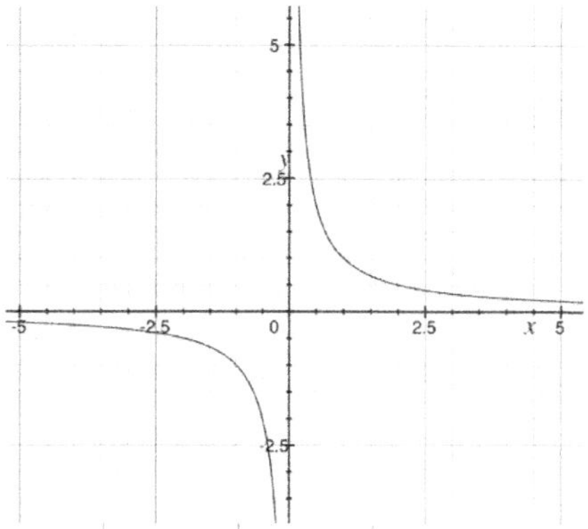

C

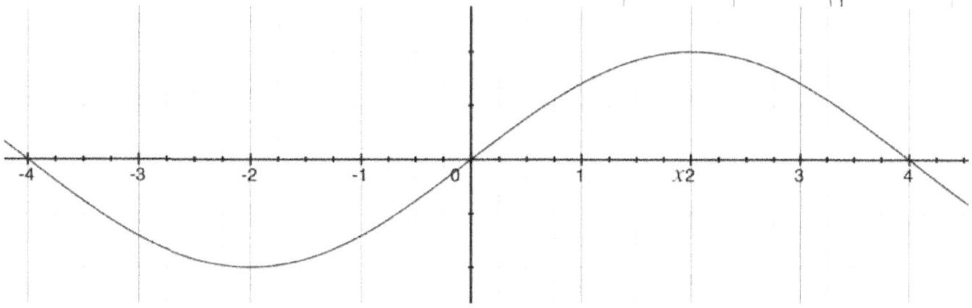

D

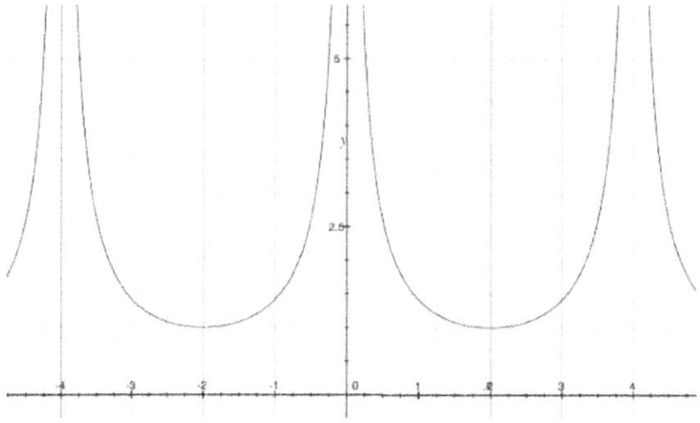

E

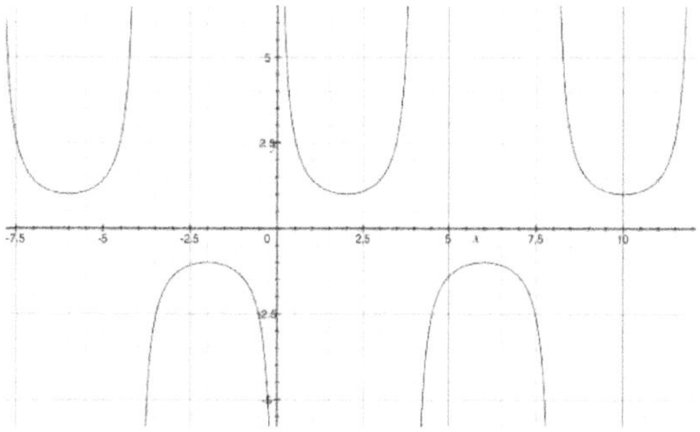

J. Suppose that a function $f(x) = ax^2 + bx + 1$ has the following property:

The area of the region between y = f(x), the x axis and the lines x = n and x = n + 1 is always greater than 1.

Which of the following is true?

A. $a > -3b$

B. $a < -9b$

C. $b < -8$

D. $a < -5$

E. $a < -2b$

2. For **ALL APPLICANTS**

A function $f(x)$ is called 'even' if $f(x) = f(-x)$ for all x and it is called 'odd' if $f(-x) = -f(x)$ for all x.

(i) Show that $f(x) = x^2$ is an even function and $g(x) = x^3$ is an odd function.

(ii) Must a polynomial be either an odd or even function? Explain your answer.

(iii) What is the only function that is both odd and even? Show that this is the only such function.

Suppose that $f(x)$ is an even function and $g(x)$ is an odd function.

(iv) Show that fg, gf and f^2 are all even functions.

Now let h(x) be some function. Define

$$f(x) = \frac{h(x) + h(-x)}{2}$$
$$g(x) = \frac{h(x) - h(-x)}{2}$$

(v) Hence show that any function can be written as the sum of an odd and an even function.

(vi) Show that every function can be written as a unique sum of an even and odd function.

Hint: What would happen if there was another expression for $h(x)$?

3. Only for **APPLICANTS IN**

- Mathematics
- Mathematics & Statistics
- Mathematics & Philosophy
- Mathematics & Computer Science

(i) Sketch the graph of $y = \frac{1}{x^2}$. Calculate $\int_1^N \frac{1}{x^2} dx$

(ii) How does $\int_1^N \frac{1}{x^2} dx$ behave as N becomes large?

(iii) Use rectangular strips to approximate and therefore calculate bounds for $\int_1^N \frac{1}{x^2} dx$

(iv) Hence show that

$$1 < \sum_{k=1}^{\infty} \frac{1}{k^2} < 2$$

(v) Show that

$$486 < 1 + \sqrt{2} + \sqrt{3} + \cdots + \sqrt{80} < 550$$

4. Only for **APPLICANTS IN**

- Mathematics
- Mathematics & Statistics
- Mathematics & Philosophy

Triangles are 'similar' if they are enlargements of each other, i.e. they are the same shape but different sizes. Figure 1 shows similar right-angled three triangles.

Let μ and λ be the scale factor of the enlargements between the triangles, such that the smallest hypotenuse is of length μc and the next largest hypotenuse is of length λc.

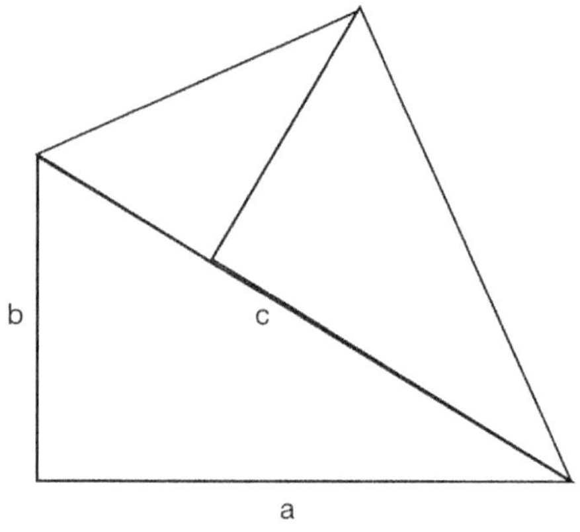

Figure 1: Not to scale

(i) Express c in terms of a, b, μ and λ.

(ii) Hence express μ and λ in terms of a, b and c.

Now suppose that the diagram can be fitted inside a circle, as shown in *Figure* 2, with the largest hypotenuse forming a diameter and each vertex on the circle.

(iii) Show that $\mu^2 + \lambda^2 = 1$

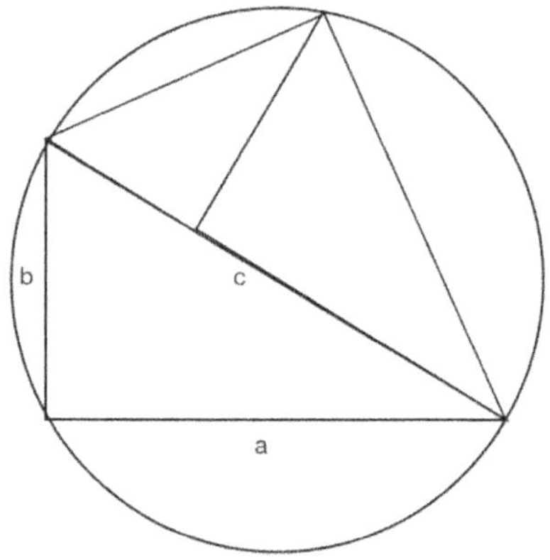

Figure 2: Not to scale

(iv) Hence find an expression for the proportion of the area of the circle taken up by the three similar triangles.

(v) Find the value of the area taken up by the triangles in the limit as a tends to b.

(vi) Suppose that in the limit as $a \to b$, we inscribe another circle inside the three similar triangles. What is the proportion of the area of the big circle taken up by the new inscribed small circle?

5. For **ALL APPLICANTS**

A city has a grid layout. A route is a series of horizontal and vertical line segments from one intersection point on the grid to another. A route cannot have any closed loops, and one cannot retrace their footsteps at any point. For example, the following depicts a route.

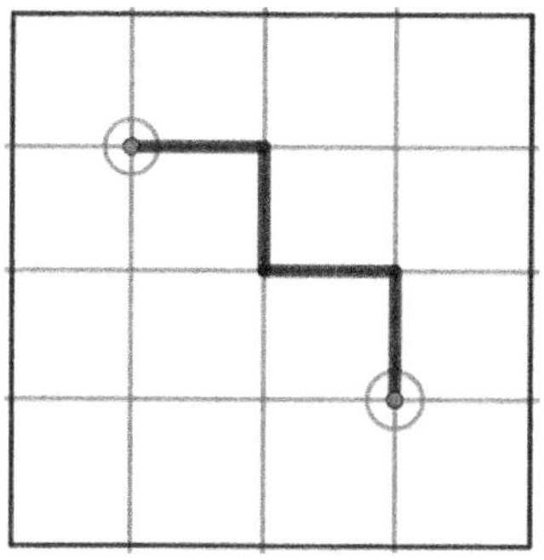

Routes start facing North (upwards on the page). The route can start with a 180-degree turn, which counts as two left turns. An (n, m) route is a route with n left turns and m right turns.

So, for example, the above route is a $(2, 1)$ route.

Suppose the city is a 2×2 grid.

(i) Find all the $(4, 1)$ routes from the top left corner to the bottom right corner. Prove that these are the only such routes.

The city is still 2×2. Suppose further that n is such that there is an $(n, 1)$ route from the top left corner to the bottom right corner.

(ii) Show that $2 < n < 12$

(iii) Show that n is either a multiple of 4 or one less than a multiple of 4.

(iv) Show that there is no $(8, 1)$ route from the top left corner to the bottom right corner.

6. Only for **APPLICANTS IN**

- Computer Science
- Mathematics & Computer Science
- Computer Science & Philosophy

(i) Express $3, 5, 7$ in the form $(n+1)^2 - n^2$.

(ii) Show that all odd numbers can be written in the form $(n+1)^2 - n^2$ by devising an algorithm for this process.

(iii) Show that if $x = (n+1)^4 - n^4$ for some integer n, then x has a factorisation $x = ab$ such that $a + b = 2(n+1)^2$.

(iv) What are the factors of 175? Hence express 175 in the form $(n+1)^4 - n^4$.

(v) Devise an algorithm for deciding whether a number can be written in the form $(n+1)^4 - n^4$ and, if so, giving the expression.

7. Only for **APPLICANTS IN**

- Computer Science
- Computer Science & Philosophy

Sentences in Martian are made up from three Martian words: *Zoop*, *Zap* and *Zeep*, according to the rule that *Zoop* and *Zeep* can never be next to each other in a sentence.

(i) List all the sentences of length 2 and all the sentences of length 3 that start with *Zap*.

Let $z(n)$ denote the number of sentences of length n. Further, let $o(n)$, $a(n)$ and $e(n)$ denote the number of sentences of length n that start with a *Zoop*, a *Zap* and a *Zeep* respectively.

(ii) Explain why $o(n) = e(n)$, $o(n) - o(n-1) = a(n-1)$ and $a(n) - a(n-1) = 2o(n-1)$ for $n > 1$.

(iii) Write down a formula for $z(n)$ in terms of $o(n)$ and $a(n)$. Hence compute $z(3)$ and $z(4)$.

A Martian sentence communicates friendship if reversing the sentence and swapping all Zoops for Zeeps (and vice versa) does not change the sentence. Let $f(n)$ be the number of friendly sentences

(iv) Show that $f(2k) = f(2k-1)$ for all positive integers k.

Hint: What must the middle word be if a sentence is friendly and has odd length?

PRACTICE PAPERS SOLUTIONS

PRACTICE PAPER 1

Question 1

A

[4 marks]

The answer is c.

$$4^{x-1} - 2^{x+1} = \frac{2^{2x}}{4} - 2(2^x) = k$$

Let $2^x = y$, then $\frac{y^2}{4} - 2y = k$. We want to find the minimum of $y^2 - 8y = 4k$, so we can initiate and set to zero to see that $y = 4$ is a stationary point. You can take the second derivative to verify that it is a minimum $(as\ 2 > 0)$ So we must have $2^x = 4 \Rightarrow x = 2$. Alternatively, you can check each option quickly to see this must be the case.

B

[4 marks]

The answer is a.

Note $\cos(x) \in \{-1.1\}$ so $\cos^2(x) \in \{0.1\}$, so $\cos(x)$ has maximum value 1. Therefore $(4 + 2 + 3)^2 = 81$ can be achieved. Note $x = 0$ gives the required value, as a sanity check.

C

[4 marks]

The answer is c.

For a line to be tangent to the circle, we need the line to intercept the circle exactly once. Consider an arbitrary line $y = \pm(x - a)$ and substitute into the equation for the circle. Expanding out the brackets, we get a quadratic equation in x: $2x^2 + (2a - 4)x + (a^2 + 3) = 0$.We require a zero discriminant which reduces to $a^2 + 4a + 2 = 0$ and solving this gives $a = -2 \pm \sqrt{2}$. Therefore, the required line is $y = \pm x \mp (-2 \pm \sqrt{2})$.

D

[4 marks]

The answer is d.

$a_1 = 2^1, a_2 = 8, a_3 = 4, a_4 = \frac{1}{2}, a_5 = \frac{1}{8}, a_6 = \frac{1}{4}, a_7 = 2$. Therefore, the sequence repeats in blocks of 6. $\frac{2019}{6} = 336$ remainder 3 so $a_{2019} = a_3 = 4$.

E

[4 marks]

The answer is c.

Note that $f(|x|-2)$ is symmetric about the y axis, so we can eliminate a, b and e. We also know that $\sqrt{2}(|\pm 2|-2)=f(0)=2$ so it cannot be d. By process of elimination, the answer is c.

F

[4 marks]

The answer is b.

To have an even number, the last digit must be either 4 or 8. For one-digit numbers, there are two possibilities, namely 4 and 8. For two-digit numbers, we can end in 4 or 8, and choose the first digit in 4 ways, so there are 4 × 2 = 8 possibilities. For three-digit numbers, there are 4 ways to choose the first digit and 3 ways to choose the second, so 4 × 3 × 2 = 24 ways. For four-digit numbers, we have 4 × 3 × 2 × 2 = 48 ways. For five-digit numbers, there is only one possibility for the fifth digit, so there are also 48 ways. Adding these together gives 130 different ways.

G

[4 marks]

The answer is c.

Consider subtracting the first equation from the second. This results in the equation $(k+1)e^y = 2k-4$ so $e^y = \frac{2k-4}{k+1}$. Since the left-hand side is positive, we require the right-hand side to also be positive. Therefore, we require $k > 2 \; or \; k < -1$. However, we also know that $e^x + e^y = 2k$. The left-hand side of this is strictly positive, so we must also have $2k > 0$. Therefore, the only valid range is $k > 2$.

H

[4 marks]

The answer is c.

$$\int_0^{\pi} g(x)g'(x)\,dx = \int_0^{\pi} g(x)\,dg(x) = \left[\frac{g^2(x)}{2}\right]_0^{\pi} = \frac{3}{2}$$

I

[4 marks]

The answer is e.

$y = \frac{\sin^2 x}{x}$ so you can immediately see that the function is odd, while graphs a-d portray even functions. Though it isn't expected, $\frac{\sin^2 x}{x}$ you can see that does indeed go through the origin by using the Maclaurin series.

J

[4 marks]

The answer is a.

We know that $A_T = \frac{1}{2} \times 15 \times 18 \times \sin 60 \frac{135\sqrt{3}}{2}$ and $A_C = 100\pi$, and $P_C = 20\pi$. Further, by the cosine rule length $xz^2 = 15^2 + 18^2 - 2 \times 15 \times 18 \times \cos 60 = 269$ Using this we get $49 < P_T < 50$. Then by process of elimination, by approximating π as 3.14 and $\sqrt{3}$ as 1.6, we can eliminate b-e leaving the answer as a.

Question 2

(i) [2 marks] Substitute into both $x = -1$ equations for y and we find that in both $y = a - b$ cases.

(ii) [5 marks] $x^3 + bx^2 - ax - 2b + 1 = bx + a$ can be written as $(x+1)(x^2 + Ax + B) = 0$ and comparing coefficients gives $A = b - 1$ and $B = 1 - a - 2b$. Three distinct points of intersection requires two real distinct solutions to $x^2 + (b-1)x + (1 - a - 2b) = 0$. Therefore, we must have a positive discriminant $(b-1)^2 - 4(1 - a - 2b) > 0$ which rearranges to $4a > -b^2 - 6b + 3$. The right-hand side is maximised when $b = -3$, which gives $4a > 12$, and subsequently $a > 3$.

(iii) [3 marks] The curves only intersect at one point if the discriminant is negative, and the quadratic contributes no other roots. We require $4a < -b^2 - 6b + 3$.

(iv) [5 marks] Let $a = \frac{3}{4}$. Then $\frac{dy}{dx} = 3x^2 + 2bx - \frac{3}{4}$ in the first case and $\frac{dy}{dx} = b$ in the second case. We require $3x^2 + 2bx - \frac{3}{4} = b$ to have one solution, and so we want the discriminant to be zero. This results in the equation $b^2 + 3b + \frac{9}{4} = 0$ and solving this gives $b = \frac{-3 \pm \sqrt{9-9}}{2} = \frac{-3}{2}$.

Question 3

(i) [2 marks]

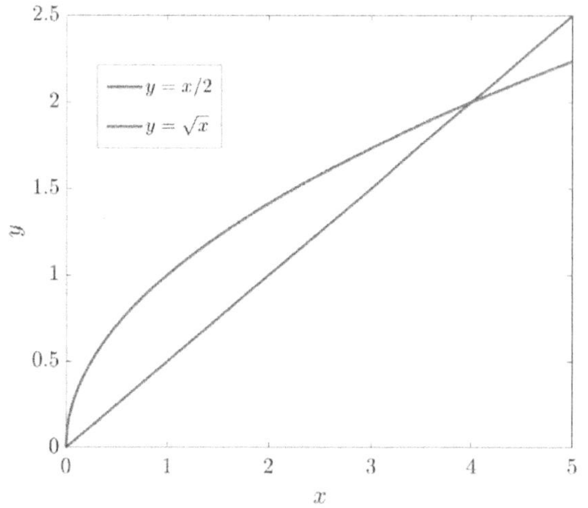

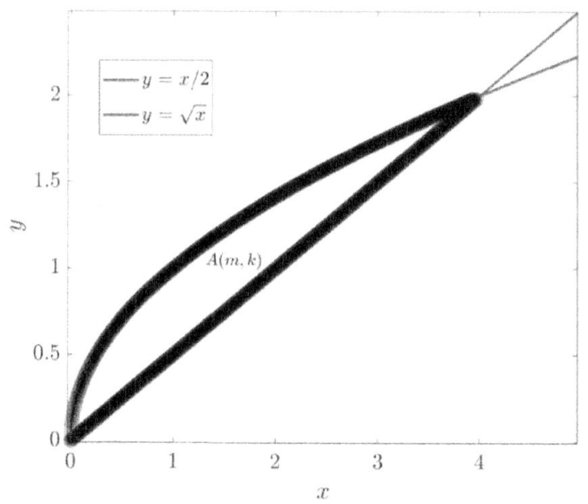

(ii) [3 marks] Intersection points are given when $\frac{1}{2}x = \sqrt{x}$ which can be rearranged to $x\left(\frac{x}{4} - 1\right) = 0$, and so the x coordinates for intersection points are $x = 0$ or $x = 4$. Substituting back into the equation, we get the y coordinates, and therefore the required coordinates of intersection points are (0, 0) and (4, 2).

(iii) [3 marks] The area between the two curves is given by $\int_0^4 x^{\frac{1}{2}} \frac{1}{2}x\,dx = \left[\frac{2}{3}x^{\frac{3}{2}} - \frac{1}{4}x^2\right]_0^4 = \frac{4}{3}$.

(iv) [5 marks] The intersection points are given when $mx = \sqrt{kx}$ so when $x(m^2x - k) = 0$. Therefore, the x coordinates for the intersection points are $x = 0$ and $x = \frac{k}{m^2}$.

$$A(m,k) = \int_0^{\frac{k}{m^2}} \sqrt{k}x^{\frac{1}{2}} - mx\,dx = \left[\frac{2}{3}\sqrt{k}x^{\frac{3}{2}} - \frac{m}{2}x^2\right]_0^{\frac{k}{m^2}} = \frac{1}{6}k^2m^{-3}$$

(v) [2 marks] $A(m,k) > km^{-2}$which can be rearranged to $k > 6m$ using the previous part of the question.

Question 4

(i) [4 marks]

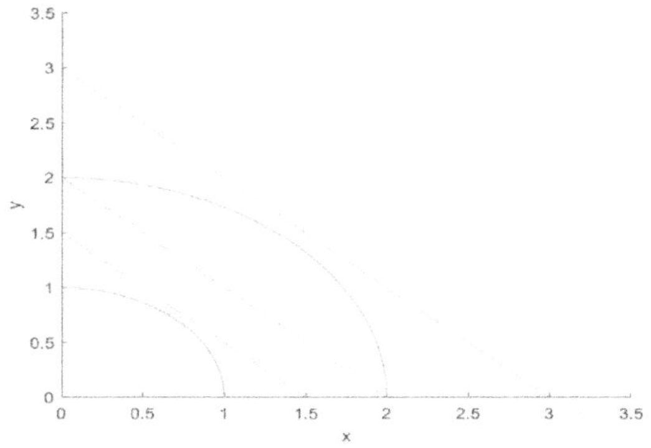

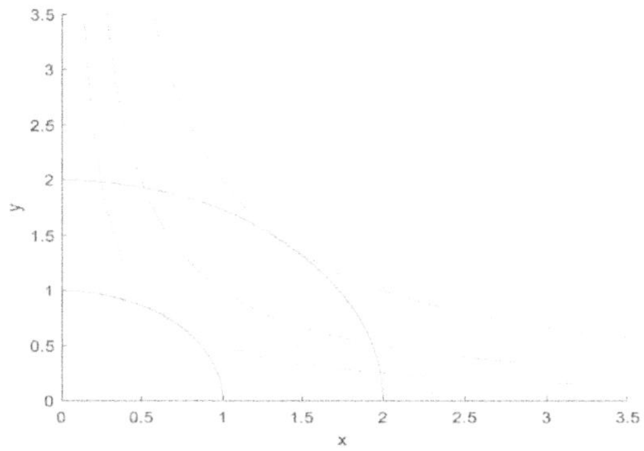

The largest value of $x + y$ occurs when the line $x + y$ is a tangent to the outer boundary of Q. The best way to see where this is achieved is noting the symmetry about the x and y axis - this means that the value will occur at $\left\{\frac{2}{\sqrt{2}}, \frac{2}{\sqrt{2}}\right\}$ i.e $\{x + y\}_{max} = 2\sqrt{2}$.

(ii) [5 marks] When looking for $\{x^2 + y^2 + 5xy\}_{max}$ we note that we want to maximise both $x^2 + y^2$ and xy, as these are all positive on the required domain we can see that this will occur on the outer boundary of Q, at $\left\{\frac{2}{\sqrt{2}}, \frac{2}{\sqrt{2}}\right\}$. Here $x^2 + y^2 = 4$ and $xy = 2$. Namely $\{x^2 + y^2 + 5xy\}_{max} = 14$.

If, we are instead considering $\{x^2 + y^2 - 4xy\}_{min}$, this will occur on the boundary, but it can't be the axes – as $x\eta = 0$ here. And note that while we want to minimise $x^2 + y^2$, it is more important to maximise $4xy$ as this term contributes more on the given domain. So, the minimum is achieved at the same point as before $\left\{\frac{2}{\sqrt{2}}, \frac{2}{\sqrt{2}}\right\}$ $an\ d\{x^2 + y^2 - 4xy\}_{min} = -4$

(iii) [6 marks] We just need to complete the square twice $x^2 + y^2 - 6x - 4y = k \Rightarrow (x-3)^2 - 9 + (y-2)^2 - 4 = k \Rightarrow (x-3)^2 + (y-2)^2 = (k + 13)$ i.e. a circle of radius $\sqrt{k+13}$ centred on (3,2). The function $x^2 + y^2 - 6x - 4y$ increases as we move away from the centre point (3,2). To see this, we can differentiate the function, but this is not necessary. The furthest point in this domain is (0,1) and we get that $\{x^2 + y^2 - 6x^{-4}y\}_{max} = 1 - 4 = -3$

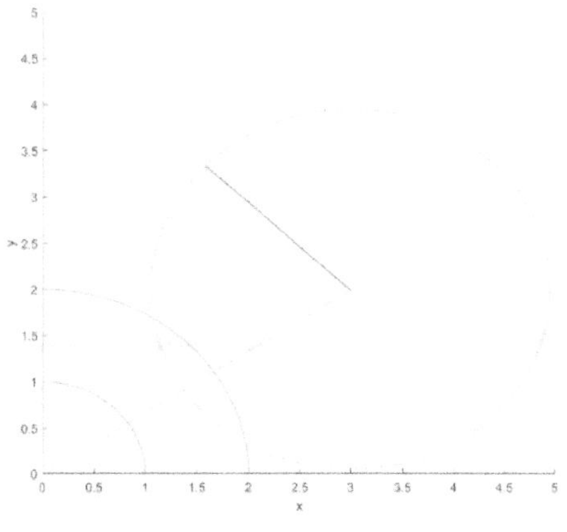

Question 5

(i) [3 marks]

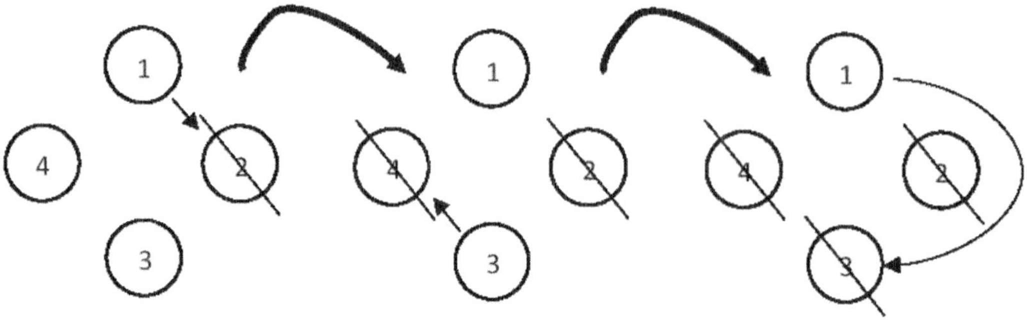

Looking at a circle of 4 soldiers, we label them $1 - 4$, and without loss of generality, start at soldier 1 and move clockwise - as indicated on the diagram. After the soldier 1 kills 2, it is the soldier 3's move, and he kills soldier 4. Now we are back to soldier 1 and he kills the soldier on his left i.e. the remaining soldier 3. Leaving soldier 1 alive. If you complete the same procedure for $n = 8$ soldiers, you will see that soldier 1, the person we start with remains alive. You should also note that after the first full rotation of the circle of soldiers, just as we get back so soldier 1, we wipe out all of the even-numbered ones.

(ii) [6 marks] We assume that the same soldier survives for n = 2k and we want to prove this is true for $n = 2k + 1$. So again, consider a circular arrangement above, that goes up to $n = 2^k + 1$. We start with soldier 1 and go round the circle once - we know that we have just taken out all of the even-numbered soldiers. Leaving soldiers $\{1, 3, 5, \dots, 2^k + 1 - 3, 2^k + 1 - 1\}$ i.e. we have $\frac{2^{k+1}}{2} = 2^k$ soldiers remaining. If we relabel each index of the soldiers by j $\rightarrow$ j+1 we are left with a circle of soldiers $\{1,2,3, \dots, 2^k - 1, 2^k\}$ and soldier 1 is starting. We know by assumption that the same soldier survives in this case - so we have proven that the same soldier (1) has survived for $n = 2^k + 1$ as well. *This is an example of proof by induction, you don't need to know this, the question walks you through it.*

(iii) [3 marks] For $n = 2^a + r$, we know that the first attacking soldier in a circle of $2a$ people survives. So, we just need to see, after r people are taken out, who the first attacking soldier is. We see that this is soldier $2r + 1$.

(iv) [3 marks] If n is a Mersenne prime then we know it can be written a $\text{n} = 2^k - 1$. To get it into a form where we can apply the results from part (iii) note that $n = 2^k - 1 = 2^{k-1} + (2^{k-1} - 1)$. This is of the form $n = 2^a + r$ where $a = k - 1$ and $r = 2^k - 1 - 1$. So, soldier $2(2^k - 1 - 1) + 1 = 2^k - 1 = n$ survives.

Question 6

(i) [2 marks] Suppose first that A is telling the truth. Then he must be a knight, contradicting the statement. Now suppose that A is lying. Then for the statement to be untrue, B has to be a knight. Therefore, A is a knave and B is a knight.

(ii) [2 marks] Condition on F. Suppose that F is a knight. Then D is a knight, and D must have said 'I am a knight'. Therefore, E says a truth and a lie which gives a contradiction. Suppose now that F is a knave. Then D is also a knave. Therefore, D said 'I am a knight'. E is telling the truth and so is a knight. Therefore, D is a knave, E is a knight and F is a knave.

(iii) [3 marks] Here we assume that 2n islanders form a circle. We label them 1 to 2n and without loss of generality start at islander 1. First, we assume the case where 1 is a knight, when they say 'the person on my right is a knave', they must be telling the truth. This means that islander 2 is a knave. When islander 2 says 'the person on my right is a knave', they must be lying - meaning islander 3 is a knight. We see that an alternating pattern forms, the knights occupy all of the odd positions, and the knaves occupy all of the even positions. We cannot have 2 knights or 2 knaves next to each other. So, in this case, we have n knights.

Similarly, if we consider the case where islander 1 is a knave, then islander 2 is a knight etc. Now all of the knaves occupy the odd positions, and all of the knights occupy the even positions. Again, we have n knights. Therefore, we must have n knights in the circle.

(iv) [2 marks] If the circle is increased to $2n + 1$ islanders. We already know that 2 knights or 2 knaves cannot be neighbours. So, say islander 1 is a knight, then the knights occupy all of the odd positions - including $2n + 1$. But as it is a circular arrangement, islander $2n + 1$ stands next to islander 1. So we arrive at a contradiction when islander $2n + 1$ says 'the person on my right is a knave', as the person to the right is islander 1, a knight. This argument follows through similarly if islander 1 is a knave, because they are not allowed to tell the truth. So this arrangement cannot occur.

(v) [3 marks] Here we make use of the fact that if we take two of these islanders at random, we can either get two knights, or a knight and a spy. If we ask them the same arbitrary question, they can either:

- Agree, in which case we know we can trust the answer, as at least one person is a knight - who always tells the truth.
- Disagree, in which case we don't know the answer; but we do know that one of the two must be a spy, as 2 knights would always agree on an answer.

If we label the islanders from 1-100, the knights know which 'number' is a spy. Take 2 islanders at random and ask them each who is the spy. If they agree and say n is the spy, then n must be the spy. If they disagree, then we know the spy must be one of the two islanders we have chosen, and the rest must be knights. So, pick one of the separated 98 islanders - which are all knights, and ask them who the spy is. They must be telling the truth. Therefore, we need at most 3 questions to identify the spy.

(vi) [3 marks] A useful observation to make, is that a spy can never identify themselves and remains unknown. This follows from the fact that: if you ask a knight, they can never identify themselves as a spy as they always tell the truth.

So the idea that exploits this fact, is that we ask each of the 100 islanders to 'write down a list of all of the spies'. We know the spies will write a list of 51 people, that will include a mix of knights and spies - but not themselves. Because as soon as they include their own name on the list, they have identified themselves as a spy. And each of the 49 knights will produce a list of 51 people that agree with each other.

We can then identify the spies as the 51 people, who are written on exactly the 49 lists that agree.

Question 7

(i) [1 mark] The list of all three letter passwords is $aaa, aab, aba, baa, abb, bab, bba, bbb$.

(ii) [2 marks] Let's say we have a password of length n. Then we can choose the first letter 2 ways - either a or b. Similarly, we can choose the second letter 2 ways, and the third etc. We see that we have a total of $2 * 2 * 2 * ... * 2 = 2^n$ possible passwords.

(iii) [2 marks] Now we are looking at the number of passwords that have no neighbouring bs, denoted C_n. We can list aa, ab, ba to give $C_2 = 3$, and aaa, aab, aba, baa, bab, to show that $C_3 = 5$.

(iv) [5 marks] With any sequence in C_{n-1}you can always add an a at the end to increase the length to n, and therefore give a unique member of C_n. This is true regardless of whether the previous letter was an a or b. So, we have C_{n-1} sequences of length n - these are the sequences that end in an a.

Now we need to find out how many legitimate sequences of length n end in a b. We note that the number of sequences in C_{n-1} that end in an a (as argued before) is C_{n-2}. To each of these sequences, we can add a b to the end of the sequence, giving a unique member of C_n. Note we have now accounted all of the sequences in C_n ending in an a or a b - these are our only possible options, so we must have them all accounted for i.e:

$$C_n = C_{n-1} + C_{n-2}$$

(v) [5 marks] The best method is to whittle down C_n. If a sequence is in C_n then we know that $C_{n-2}(= C_n - C_{n-1})$ end in a b. So, we eliminate these. By symmetry in a and b we know that C_{n-2} must start in b, so we also eliminate these. Note we have been too zealous with our eliminations! We have taken away the sequences that start and end in b twice. So, we need to enumerate how many of these there are and add them back in.

If we look at the sequences:

$$ba|ab|ab$$
$$ba|ba|ab$$
$$ba|aa|ab$$

we see that we need a sequence that looks like

$$ba|C_{n-4}|ab$$

Searching for sequences of length n that starts and ends in a b, we know there are C_{n-4} of these (it is a good job that we have $n \geq 5$). So we have:

$$P_n = C_n - 2C_{n-2} + C_{n-4}$$

PRACTICE PAPER 2

Question 1

A

[4 marks]

The answer is b.

The cubic can be factorised as follows: $(x - 1)(x - 2)(x - 3)$. The curve is a positive cubic, upon sketching we see that we have a positive contribution between $x = 1$ and $x = 2$, and we need to take into consideration the negative area between $x = 2$ and $x = 3$. We calculate the total area as

$$\int_1^2 x^3 - 6x^2 + 11x - 6\,dx - \int_2^3 x^3 - 6x^2 + 11x - 6\,dx$$

B

[4 marks]

The answer is d.

The quadratic is only positive for $1 < x < 2$ so f is only defined on this interval. The quadratic is zero at $x = 1$ and $x = 2$ so f tends to negative infinity here. Upon differentiating the quadratic, we see we have a maximum value of 1 at $x = \frac{3}{2}$. So, the maximum value of ln $(-4x^2 + 12x - 8)_{max} = \ln 1 = 0$

C

[4 marks]

The answer is c.

$f(x) = 0 \Rightarrow 16x^4 + 32x^3 + 24x^2 + 8x^{+1} = x^4 \Rightarrow (2x + 1)^4 = x^4$. This means that $2x + 1 = \pm x \Rightarrow x = -\frac{1}{3}$ or -1

D

[4 marks]

The answer is c.

Substituting the function into the differential equation gives $k^2 + k = 1$ which has a strictly positive discriminant.

E

[4 marks]

The answer is a.

Evaluating the first few terms $(1,1,2,4,7,11,16)$ shows that the pattern is a difference that increases by one each term. This suggests the following formula:$a_n = 1 + 1 + 2 + 3 + \ldots + (n - 2)$. This is one plus an arithmetic series so $a_n = 1 + (n - 1)(n - 2)/2$. Therefore $a_{100} = 4852$.

F

[4 marks]

The answer is d.

The identity $cos^2x + sin^2x = 1$ transforms the equation to the following cubic in cos x: $4cos^3x - 8cos^2x + 5cosx - 1 = 0$. By the factor theorem, $cos\ x - 1$ is a factor. The cubic factorises to $2(2cosx - 1)(cosx - 1) = 0$.

$cosx = 1/2$ has two solutions in the given range and $cosx = 1$ has one solution. So, in total there are 3 solutions in this range.

G

[4 marks]

The answer is b.

The roots are exactly the integers, which rules out c) and d). And note that as x gets large in magnitude, the maximum value of y should increase in both directions - due to the factor of $(x - 2)^2$ and the fact that $|sin(\pi x)| \leq 1$. So we can rule out a) and e).

H

[4 marks]

The answer is c.

Adding I to each side gives a binomial expansion on the left-hand side: $(e^x - 2)^4 = 1$. Thus $e^x - 2 = 1$ or $e^x - 2 = -1$, giving two valid values for $e^x (> 0)$.

I

[4 marks]

The answer is c.

Observe that $2^{n+1} - 1 = 2^n + 2^n - 1 + \ldots + 2 + 1 = 2(2(2(\ldots(2 + 1) + 1) + 1 + \ldots + 1)$ where there are n lots of 2 (and n lots of $+1$).$f(2x + 1) = -f(x) so f[2(2(2(\ldots(2 + 1) + 1) + 1 + \ldots + 1)] = -1^n$. Thus $f(2^n + 1 - 1) = -1^n$. Therefore $f(2^7 - 1) + f(2^6 - 1) = -1^6 + -1^5 = 1 - 1 = 0$.

J

[4 marks]

The answer is a.

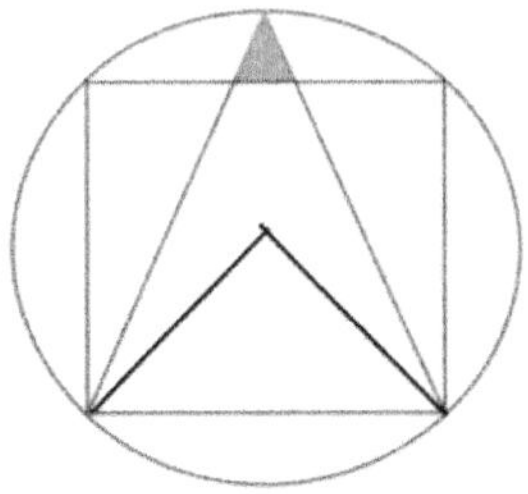

By Pythagoras on the bold right-angle triangle, the side length of the square is 2. The height of the shaded triangle is therefore $\sqrt{2}-1$, and the height of the large triangle is $1 + \sqrt{2}$. Considering their respective angles, note that the small and large triangles are similar with a scale factor of $\frac{\sqrt{2}-1}{\sqrt{2}+1}$. Half the base of the small triangle is therefore equal to $\frac{\sqrt{2}-1}{\sqrt{2}+1}$, so the small triangle has area $\left(\sqrt{2}-1\right) * \frac{\sqrt{2}-1}{\sqrt{2}+1}$

Question 2

(i) [2 marks] $x_1 = 11^{x_2} = 2, x^3 = \frac{3}{2}, x_4 = \frac{5}{3}, x_5 = \frac{8}{5}$. Thus the product $x_1x_2x_3x_4x_5 = 8$.

(ii) [3 marks] By inspection $(u_n) = 1,1,2,3,5,8, \ldots$ i.e. the Fibonacci sequence. We see that $u_n = u_{n-1} + u_{n-2}$ for $n \geq 3$, or equivalently $u_{n+2} = u_{n+1} + u_n$ for $n \geq 1$.

(iii) [4 marks] If $u_n = p^n$ then applying (ii) gives $p^{n+2} = p^{n+1} + p^n$. Noting that $p \neq 0$ we arrive at $p^2 - p - 1 = 0$. This has solutions $p_1 = \frac{1+\sqrt{5}}{2}$ and $p_2 = \frac{1-\sqrt{5}}{2}$.

(iv) [4 marks] Setting $n = 1$ gives $1 = c_1\frac{1+\sqrt{5}}{2} + c_2\frac{1-\sqrt{5}}{2}$. Letting $n = 2$ gives $1 = c_1\frac{3+\sqrt{5}}{2} + C_2\frac{3-\sqrt{5}}{2}$. Solving simultaneously gives $c_1 = \frac{1}{\sqrt{5}}$ and $c_2 = -\frac{1}{\sqrt{5}}$. It remains to show that $u_{n+2} = u_{n+1} + u_n$ for $n \geq 1$, it is simple to plug in and check this.

(v) [2 marks] Cancelling diagonally, $x_1x_2x_3x_4 \ldots x_n = u_{n+1}$ which upon using the previous results is:

$$\frac{1}{\sqrt{5}}\left(\frac{1+\sqrt{5}}{2}\right)^{n+1} - \frac{1}{\sqrt{5}}\left(\frac{1-\sqrt{5}}{2}\right)^{n+1}$$

Question 3

(i) [5 marks]

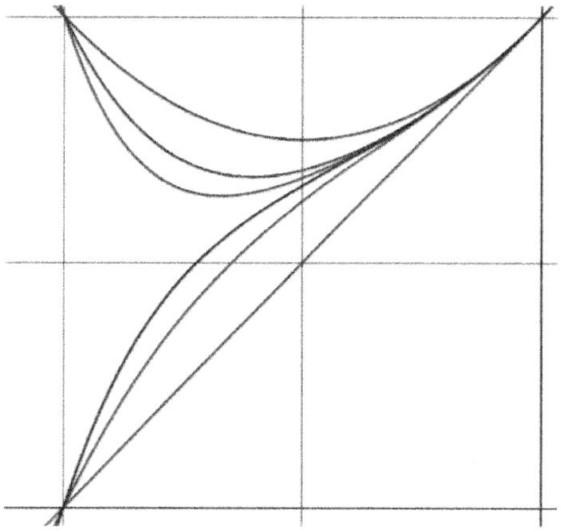

$k = 1$ and $k = 2$ give familiar curves. Following the hint $f_{k+2}(x) - f_k(x) = x^{k+1}(x+1)$ which, in this range, is positive for odd k and negative for even k. Thus, the curves for even k values are a series of "downwards stretched" curves and the curves for odd k values are curves successively stretched upwards from $y = 1 + x$.

(ii) [5 marks] Using the same observation, the area will be:

- $\int_{-1}^{0} f_{k+2}(x) - f_k(x)\,dx$ for odd values of k.
- $\int_{-1}^{0} f_k(x)\,dx - f_{k+2}(x)$ for even values of k.

Thus, in general we have

$$\int_{-1}^{0} (-1)^{k+1}\left(f_{k+2}(x) - f_k(x)\right)dx = \int_{-1}^{0} (-1)^{k+1}\left(x^{k+2} + x^{k+1}\right)dx = \frac{1}{(k+2)(k+3)}$$

(iii) [3 marks]

$$A(k) = \sum_{k=1}^{n} \frac{1}{(k+2)(k+3)} = \sum_{k=1}^{n} \frac{1}{k+1} - \frac{1}{k+2} - \frac{1}{k+3} = \frac{1}{3} - \frac{1}{n+3}$$

Where we see the last equality comes from expanding out the sum, and seeing that all but the first and last terms cancel. We can conclude that$lim_n \to \infty A(n) = \frac{1}{3}$.

(iv) [2 marks] As one adds more graphs of $y = f_k(x)$ to the above diagram, more non-overlapping segments are added (between successive "even" and "odd" curves). The total of these segments becomes increasingly close to the area of the region between $y = 1 + x + x^2$, $y = 1 + x$ and $x = -1$. Thus the area in question is $\frac{1}{3}$.

Question 4

(i) [2 marks] Using trigonometric relations on triangle POR, we can see that R is located at $(0, tan\ \alpha)$. The gradient of the line is $\frac{-\tan\alpha}{1} - \tan\alpha$. The equation of the line is $y - 0 = -tan\alpha(x-1)$ which simplifies to $y = -tan\alpha(x-1)$.

(ii) [3 marks] We know that the gradient of this line will be $\tan\theta$. Since the line goes through the origin, the equation of the line is $y = xtan\theta$.

To find the coordinates of Q, we calculate the point of intersection between the two lines. $xtan\theta = -tan\alpha(x-1)$ and solving for x gives $x = \frac{\tan\alpha}{\tan\theta + \tan\alpha}$. The y coordinate is $y = \frac{\tan\theta\tan\alpha}{\tan\theta+\tan\alpha}$.

(iii) [3 marks] The simplest example of when $A(\alpha,\theta) = B(\alpha,\theta)$ is when triangle POQ is isosceles and the line OR bisects PQ. This occurs when $\alpha = \frac{\pi}{4}$ and $\theta = \frac{\pi}{4}$.

The area of triangle POQ can be calculated using $A = \frac{1}{2}bh$ where b is the base and h the height of the triangle. In this case $b = 1$ and $h = tan\alpha$ so $A(POQ) = \frac{1}{2}tan\alpha$. We want $A(\alpha,\theta)$ to be equal to exactly half this area, so $A(\alpha,\theta) = \frac{1}{4}tan\alpha$ which is independent of θ .

(iv) [4 marks] We first calculate the length OQ Pythagoras. $|OQ|^2 = \left(\frac{\tan\theta\tan\alpha}{\tan\theta+\tan\alpha}\right)^2 + \left(\frac{\tan\alpha}{\tan\theta+\tan\alpha}\right)^2 = \frac{\tan^2\alpha(1+\tan^2\theta)}{(\tan\theta+\tan\alpha)^2} = \frac{\tan^2\alpha\sec^2\theta}{(\tan\theta+\tan\alpha)^2}$. Then we can determine the area of the triangle using $A = \frac{1}{2}ab\sin C$. In this case, $A(\alpha,\theta) = \frac{1}{2}{}^{x}\sqrt{\frac{\tan^2 a\sec^2\theta}{(\tan\theta+\tan\alpha)^2}} \times \sin\theta\ \bar{r}\frac{\cot\theta\tan\sigma}{2(\tan\theta+\tan\alpha)}$.

(v) [3 marks] When $\alpha = \frac{\pi}{4}$, $A\left(\frac{\pi}{4},\theta\right)$. The area of triangle POR is $\frac{1}{2}$ when $\alpha = \frac{\pi}{4}$. For $A\left(\frac{\pi}{4},\theta\right) = \frac{1}{2}B\left(\frac{\pi}{4},\theta\right)$, we want $A\left(\frac{\pi}{4},\theta\right) = \frac{1}{6}$. Then we must have $\frac{1}{6} = \frac{1}{2\tan\theta(1+\tan\theta)}$. This simplifies to the quadratic $\tan^2\theta + \tan\theta - 3 = 0$ and solving for $\tan\theta$ gives $\tan\theta = \frac{-1\pm\sqrt{1-4(-3)}}{2} = \frac{-1\pm\sqrt{13}}{2}$. For $0 < \theta < \frac{\pi}{2}$, we must have $\tan\theta = \frac{-1+\sqrt{73}}{2}$.

Question 5

(i) [3 marks] By inspection we have:

- $n = 3$ with $x = 2$
- $n = 4$ with $x = 3$
- $n = 5$ with $x = 2, 3, 4$
- $n = 6$ with $x = 5$

(ii) [4 marks] x can be any integer from 2 to $n - 1$ which does not share a common factor with n (i.e. coprime). Any value of x that isn't coprime with n results in closed loops that miss out on some children.

(iii) [3 marks] There are $n - 2$ possible values if n is prime because, by definition, none of the integers from 2 to $n - 1$ have a factor in common with n.

(iv) [5 marks] Noting that $5040 = 7! = 1 * 2 * 3 * 4 * 5 * 6 * 7 sox \geq 8$. 8 and 5040 have the factors 2 and 4 in common so x cannot be 8.9 and 5040 have the factor 3 in common so x cannot be 3.10 and 5040 have the factors 2 and 5 in common so x cannot be 10. 11 is prime and 5040 is not divisible by 11 so 11 is a possible value of x. Thus, it is the smallest possible value of x.

Question 6

(i) [2 marks] First let us condition on the card that A receives. Let's assume it is the truth card. This implies that B has the liar card and it is a Monday. But this means that both of person B's statements are lies, which is a contradiction - as they can only tell exactly one lie. So, A must have the liar card.

(ii) [5 marks] Exactly the same line of reasoning holds and shows that A must have the liar card. If person B has a truth card then all of B's statements are true and, provided it isn't Monday, exactly one of A's statements is a lie - so this situation is consistent. If person B has a liar card then B's second statement is a lie, so B's first statement is true which gives, as desired, that A has a liar card. Person A is then telling exactly one lie, as desired, provided it isn't Monday. Therefore, B can have either card.

(iii) [3 marks] If C has a truth card then B must have a liar card. If C has a liar card then C's second statement is the lie so "B has a liar card" is true. Therefore, B has a liar card.

(iv) [5 marks] D's first statement is an obvious lie so D has a liar card and it is before 2pm. This makes B a liar, so it is true that exactly one person has a truth card. Suppose that C has a truth card. Then A has a truth card. This contradicts B's true statement, so C has a liar card. Thus, by elimination, A must have the only truth card.

Question 7

B

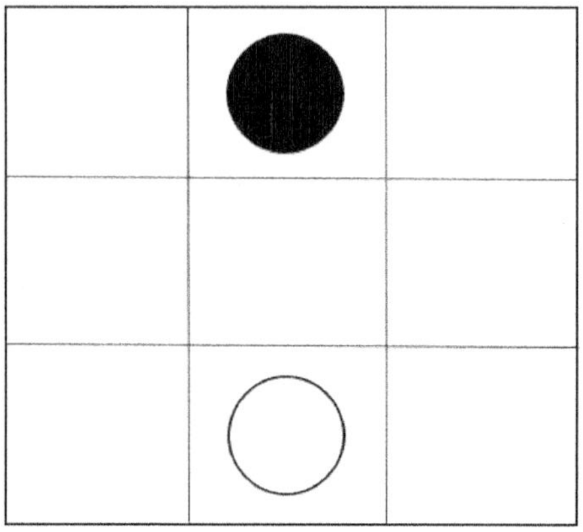

A

(i) [2 marks]

If A goes left or right B can go any of left, right or down. If A goes up B can go left or right. Thus, there are $2 * 3 + 1 * 2 = 8$possible sequences for the first two moves.

(ii) [3 marks] No - after B's first move, they can be in the top left, top right or centre square. After one move A can only be in the bottom left, bottom right or centre square. A cannot move from any of these squares to any of the top left, top right or centre square.

(iii) [3 marks] If A goes left or right A has two options for their next move: up or right. If A goes up A has three options for their next move: left or right or up. Hence there are $2 * 3 * 2 + 1 * 2 * 3 = 18$ possible three move sequences for the first three total moves.

(iv) [2 marks] Considering the 18 options above; A can only win if A moves up twice and B moves left or right on their first move. Whereas B can only be in the top left, top right or centre square after the first three moves, so cannot win within 3 total moves.

(v) [1 mark] By part (iv) we see that A should move up on their first move.

(vi) [1 mark] B cannot win in the case A moves up 1 square first. As B is blocked from progressing to the centre square, they must move left or right - allowing A to win with their next move (upwards).

(vii) [3 marks] Player A does not necessarily win. B can make judicious moves only to the right and left (staying on row $2n$) waiting for A to get to the row $2n - 1$, then "follow" A so B is constantly blocking A. In order to get into this position, B needs to not be in the same column as A after A has done their final move to get to row $2n - 1$, but 1 column either to the left or right. B can always position themselves like this in order for their next move to be a blocking one.

PRACTICE PAPER 3

Question 1

A

[4 marks]

The answer is d.

$$\sum_{k=0}^{\infty}\frac{3^{k+1}-2^k}{6^k}=\sum_{k=0}^{\infty}\frac{3^{k+1}}{3^k\times 2^k}-\frac{2^k}{3^k\times 2^k}=\sum_{k=0}^{\infty}\frac{3}{2^k}-\frac{1}{3^k}=\frac{3}{1-\frac{1}{2}}-\frac{1}{1-\frac{1}{3}}=\frac{9}{2}$$

B

[4 marks]

The answer is c.

$\log_{x^2+1}(3x^2+7)=2$ and using logarithm laws, this becomes $(x^2+1)^2=3x^2+7$. This can be rearranged to $x^4-x^2-6=0$. Let $y=x^2>0$, then $y^2-y-6=0$, so $(y-3)(y-2)=0$. Therefore $y=3$ or $y=-2$, the latter of which contradicts the statement $y>0$. Therefore $x=\pm\sqrt{y}=\pm\sqrt{3}$.

C

[4 marks]

The answer is e.

$x^2-6x+y^2-4y+9=0$ can be rewritten as $(x-3)^2+(y-2)^2=4$ which is the equation of a circle of radius 2 and with centre $(3,2)$. We consider where the line connecting the centre of the circle and the origin $y=2x$ meets the circle itself since this will give the x co-ordinate nearest the origin. Therefore, we must solve $(x-3)^2+(2x-2)^2=4$. We can expand this out and solve using the quadratic formula, giving

D

[4 marks]

The answer is b.

Using double angle formulae, we can write $\sin x=2\sin\left(\frac{x}{2}\right)\cos\left(\frac{x}{2}\right)$. Then our equation becomes $2\sqrt{2}\sin\left(\frac{x}{2}\right)\cos\left(\frac{x}{2}\right)=2\cos\left(\frac{x}{2}\right)$. Therefore either $\cos\left(\frac{x}{2}\right)=0$ or $\sqrt{2}sin\left(\frac{x}{2}\right)-1=0$. Solving in the first case gives $x=\pi,3\pi$, ... and solving in the second case gives $\frac{x}{2}=\frac{\pi}{4}$, ... so the smallest possible root is $\frac{\pi}{2}$. We can equally just check all of the options in turn to see this.

E

[4 marks]

The answer is c.

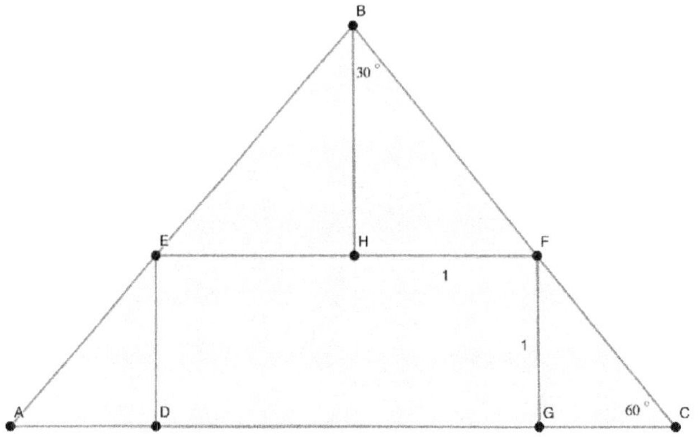

Figure 1: Not to scale

Let $AB = x$, $BF = y$ and $FC = z$. Then $x = y + z$. Looking at triangle BHF and using the fact that $HF = 1$, we can calculate $\sin 30 = \frac{1}{y} = 2$, so $y = 2$. Similarly, looking at triangle FGC, we calculate $\sin 60 = \frac{1}{z}$ so $z = \frac{2}{\sqrt{3}}$. Therefore, the total perimeter is $3x = 6 + 2\sqrt{3}$.

F

[4 marks]

The answer is d.

We know that $(x^3 + 3)$ is a factor of $g(f(x))$ which implies that $x + 3$ is a factor of $g(x)$. So in particular, we have that $g(-3) = 0 \Rightarrow (-1)^n - (-2)^n(-2)^n = 0$. We see general even and odd values of n do not work. Plugging in values for $n = 0, -1$, we see that both are valid solutions.

G

The answer is b.

We see that the y intercept is positive so we can rule out a). When x is small, we want the graph to look like $c - dx$ where c, d are positive constants. This leaves us with b) or d). Note that for $x \geq 0$ d) is always positive. This can be seen by factoring as follows: $x^4(x - 1) + x(x - 3) + 3$. So the answer must be b).

H

[4 marks]

The answer is a.

$$y = -x^4 + 2bx^3 + 6ax^2 - x + 3$$
$$\Rightarrow y' = -4x^3 + 6bx^2 + 12ax - 1$$
$$\Rightarrow y'' = -12x^2 + 12bx + 12a$$

We require $y'' < 0$ for a maximum to occur i.e. we want a negative discriminant for $-x^2 + bx + a < 0 \Rightarrow b^2 + 4a < 0 \Rightarrow b^2 < -4a$.

I

[4 marks]

The answer is d.

Note $2x^2 - x + 1$ is symmetric about $x = \frac{1}{4}$ so in $(2x^2 - x + 1)$ is symmetric about $x = \frac{1}{4}$. We want the integrals either side of this to cancel out, so we need $\sin(k\pi x)\cos^{(k\pi x)}(= \frac{1}{2}\sin(2k\pi x))$ to be an odd function about $x = \frac{1}{4}$. This only happens for even k.

J

[4 marks]

The answer is d.

The best method is to simply calculate u_n up to $u_{10} = 4093$. Noting that $2^{12} = 4096$. Nothing that $2^{12} = 4096$ and that adding all previous values with $n = 0, 1, \ldots, 10$, we see that if we add less terms we don't reach 2^{12}.

Another way to tackle this question is to find the general formula: $u_n = 2^{n+1} - 3$, we do this by substituting in u_{n-1} then u_{n-2}, all the way to $u_0 = 1$. Then we get (after summing a geometric series)

$$\sum_{n=0}^{k} u_n = 2^{k+3} - 3k - 7$$

We see that we have to have k = 10 as the first instance where this is true.

Question 2

(i) [2 marks] Let c denote the current age of the mathematician. Then we have $c + n^3 = a^3$ for some positive integer a. Rearranging gives:

$$c = a^3 - n^3 = (a - n)(a^2 + an + n^2)$$

(ii) [3 marks] For the current age c to be prime, the smaller factor must be equal to 1 i.e. $a - n \Rightarrow a = n + 1$. Expanding the previous expression gives:

$$c = (n + 1)^2 + n(n + 1) + n^2 = 3n^2 + 3n + 1$$

(iii) [5 marks] Let a denote a number which is a perfect square and a perfect cube. $a = b^3 = d^2 = \left(p_1^{s_1} * p_2^{s_2} * \ldots * p_n^{s_n}\right)^3 = \left(q_1^{r_1} * q_2^{r_2} * \ldots * q_m^{r_m}\right)^2$ where p_i and q_i are prime factors. So

$$p_1^{3s_1} * p_2^{3s_2} * \ldots * p_n^{3s_n} = q_1^{2r_1} * q_2^{2r_2} * \ldots * q_m^{2r_m}$$

Note p_i and q_i must be the same due to prime factorisation property (otherwise it would contradict the equality). So $m = n$ and $p_i = q_i$. Powers on the left-hand side are divisible by 3 and powers on the right-hand side are divisible by 2, which implies that the powers are divisible by 6 i.e.

$$a = (p_1^{t_1} * p_2^{t_2} * \ldots * p_n^{t_n})^6$$

(iv) [5 marks] Using (i)

$$\sum_{n=1}^{k} 3n^2 + 3n + 1 = \sum_{n=1}^{k} (a - n)\,(a^2 + \text{an} + n^2) = \sum_{n=1}^{k} a^3 - n^3 = \sum_{n=1}^{k} (n + 1)^3 - n^3$$

Calculating a few terms, we see this is a telescoping sum and are left with

$$\sum_{n=1}^{k} 3n^2 + 3n + 1 = (k + 1)^3 - 1$$

Using a few common arithmetic sequences $\sum n = \frac{1}{2}k(k - 1)$ and $\sum 1 = k$. We rearrange to give:

$$3\sum_{n=1}^{k} n^2 = (k + 1)^3 - 1 - \frac{3}{2}k(k - 1) - k \Rightarrow \sum_{n=1}^{k} n^2 = \frac{k(k + 1)(2k + 1)}{6}$$

Question 3

(i) [2 marks] Set $y = -x$ in I. $Then\ f(0) = f(x) + f(-x)$. Set $y = 0$ in 2. Then $f(0) = af(0)$ for any positive, real a. Hence, we must have $f(0) = 0$. Therefore $f(x) + f(-x) = 0$ and rearranging gives the desired result.

(ii) [2 marks] $f(\pi) = [\pi] = 4$ and so $f(\pi) + f(\pi) = 8$.

However, $f(\pi + \pi) = f(2\pi) = [2\pi] = 7$ and so $f(x + y) \neq f(x) + f(y)$.

(iii) [4 marks] $\int_0^{10} f(x)\,dx = \int_0^1 f(x)\,dx + \int_1^2 f(x)\,dx + \cdots + \int_9^{10} f(x)\,dx = \left[\frac{f(1)+f(0)}{2}\right] \times 1 + \left[\frac{f(2)+f(1)}{2}\right] \times 1 + \cdots + \left[\frac{f(10)+f(9)}{2}\right] \times 1 = \left[\frac{f(1)+0}{2}\right] \times 1 + \left[\frac{2f(1)-0+f(1)}{2}\right] \times 1 + \cdots + \left[\frac{10f(1)+9f(1)}{2}\right] x^1 = \frac{f(1)}{2} + \frac{3f(1)}{2} + \cdots + \frac{19f}{2} = \frac{f(1)}{2} \Sigma_{k=0}^{9} 2k + 1 = 50f(1)$ using property 2 in the intermediate step.

(iv) [4 marks] Since we are using an arbitrary number of trapezia, we set $10 = l \times h$. Then we can write $\int_0^{10} f(x)\,dx = \int_0^h f(x)dx + \int_h^{2h} f(x)\,dx + \cdots + \int_{(l-1)h}^{lh} f(x)\,dx = \left[\frac{f(h)+f(0)}{2}\right] \times h + \left[\frac{f(2n)+f(n)}{2}\right] \times h + \cdots + \left[\frac{f(lh)+f((l-1)h)}{2}\right] x^h = \frac{h}{2}\left[hf(1) + 3hf(1) + \cdots 19h_f(1)\right] = \frac{h^2 f(1)}{2} \Sigma_{k=0}^{l-1} 2k + 1 = \frac{h^2 f(1)}{2} \times \frac{1}{2} \times (1 + 2l - 1) \times l = \frac{h^2 l^2 f(1)}{2}$. Then this simplifies to $50f(1)$.

(v) [3 marks] $\int_{-10}^{-5} f(x)\,dx = \int_{10}^{5} f(-y)\,dy$ using change of variables $y = -x$ in the integral. Using part (i), this becomes $-\int_5^{10} f(y)\,dy = \left[-\int_0^{16} f(y)\,dy + \int_0^5 f(y)\,dy\right] = -50(1) + \frac{25}{5} f(1) = \frac{75}{5} f(1)$ where the second integral was calculated using the same method as in part (iii).

Question 4

(i) [2 marks]

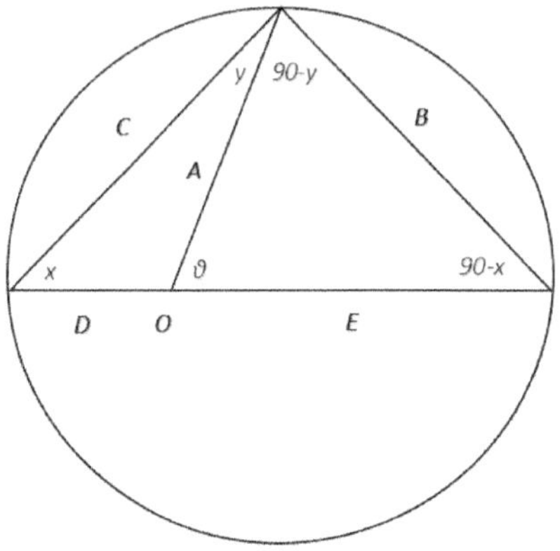

Note $\angle CB = 90$ by the diameter circle theorem. And $\angle AD = 180 - (x + y)$. This implies that $\angle AE = 180 - (180 - (x + y)) = x + y$. So we can conclude that

$$\theta = x + y$$

(ii) [3 marks] The sine rule tells us that $\frac{\sin A}{A} = \frac{\sin B}{B} = \frac{\sin C}{C}$. Noting that $sin(90 - x) = cos(x)$, $cos(90 - x) = sin(x)$ and $\angle EB = 180 - (90 - y) - (x + y) = 90 - x$. We can apply the sine rule to give

$$\frac{\sin(90 - x)}{A} = \frac{\sin(x + y)}{B} \Rightarrow \frac{A}{B}\sin(x + y)$$

(iii) [4 marks] We utilise the identity $\sin^2 z + \cos^2 z = 1$ for all z. Looking at the triangle made up of sides ADC , applying the sine rule and using properties of sin gives

$$\frac{\sin x}{A} = \frac{\sin(x + y)}{C}$$

Upon using the identity and (ii) we get the required result

$$1 = \left(\frac{A^2}{B^2} + \frac{A^2}{C^2}\right)\sin^2(x + y) \Rightarrow \sin^2(x + y) = \frac{B^2C^2}{A^2(B^2 + C^2)}$$

(iv) [2 marks] The left triangle has area $A_1 = \frac{1}{2}AC\sin(y)$ and the right triangle has area $A_2 = \frac{1}{2}AB\cos(y)$. Equating these and rearranging gives the condition

$$\tan y = \frac{B}{C}$$

(v) [4 marks] $\tan y = \frac{6}{8} \Rightarrow \cos y = \frac{8}{10}$ for the areas of the triangle to be equal. Looking at the whole triangle - we see that $tan\ x = \frac{6}{8}$ also. This means that $x = y$ in this domain, and, in particular, that the triangle made up of sides DAC is isosceles; with $D = A$. The cosine rule on the triangle with sides DAC gives:

$$D^2 = A^2 + 64 - 16A\cos y \Rightarrow D^2 = D^2 + 64 - 16D \times \frac{4}{5}$$

Rearranging gives $D = 5\ cm$.

Question 5

(i) [1 mark] $F_0 = 0, F_1 = 1, F_2 = 1, F_3 = 2, F_4 = 3$

(ii) [2 marks] Let $F_n = \lambda^n$. Then $\lambda^n = \lambda^{n-1} + \lambda^{n-2}$ which reduces to the quadratic $\lambda^2 - \lambda - 1 = 0$. Solving for λ using the quadratic formula gives $\lambda_{\pm} = \frac{1 \pm \sqrt{5}}{2}$.

(iii) [2 marks] Write $F_0 = A + B = 0$ so $A = -B$. Then $F_1 = 1 = A\lambda_+ + B\lambda_- = A(\lambda_+ - \lambda_-)$. Therefore $A = \frac{1}{\lambda_+ - \lambda_-} = \frac{1}{\sqrt{5}}$. Substituting this in gives $F_n = \frac{1}{\sqrt{5}}\left[\left(\frac{1+\sqrt{5}}{2}\right)^n + \left(\frac{1-\sqrt{5}}{2}\right)^n\right]$ as required.

(iv) [4 marks] Let $S(k+1) = \sum_{n=0}^{k} F_n = \frac{1}{\sqrt{5}} \sum_{n=0}^{k} \lambda_+^n - \lambda_-^n$ which is the sum of two geometric series. Therefore $S(k+1) = \frac{1}{\sqrt{5}}\left[\frac{1-\lambda_+^{k-1}}{\lambda_-} - \frac{1-\lambda_-^{k+1}}{\lambda_t}\right] = \frac{1}{\lambda_+ \lambda_- \sqrt{5}}\left[\lambda + (1 - \lambda_+^{k+1}) - \lambda_-(1 - \lambda_-^{k+1})\right] = \frac{-1}{\sqrt{5}}\left[\lambda_-^{k+2} - \lambda_+^{k+2} + \lambda_+ - \lambda_-\right] = \frac{1}{\sqrt{5}}\left[\lambda_-^{k+2} - \lambda_+^{k+2}\right] - 1 = F_{k+2} - 1$.

(v) [3 marks] $G_0 = 1, G_1 = 3, G_n = G_{n-1} + G_{n-2}$. Let $G_n = \lambda^n$. Substituting in and solving for λ gives $\lambda_{\pm} = \frac{1 \pm \sqrt{5}}{2}$ as before. Write $G_n = A\lambda_+^n + B\lambda_-^n$ then G_0. Furthermore, $G_1 = 3 = (1 - B)\lambda_+ + B\lambda_-$ and solving for B gives $B = \frac{3-\lambda_+}{\lambda_- - \lambda_+} = \frac{\lambda_+ - 3}{\sqrt{5}}$ and $A = \frac{3-\lambda_-}{\sqrt{5}}$. Then $G_n = \frac{3-\lambda_-}{\sqrt{5}}\lambda_+^n + \frac{3-\lambda_+}{\lambda_- - \lambda_+}\lambda_-^n$ gives the expression for G.

(vi) [3 marks] Let $L(k+1) = \sum_{n=0}^{k} G_n$ then $L(k+1) = A\sum_{n=0}^{k} \lambda_+^n + B\Sigma_{n=0}^{4} \lambda_-^n = A\left(\frac{1-\lambda_+^{k-1}}{1-\lambda_+}\right) + B\left(\frac{1-\lambda_-^{k-1}}{1-\lambda_-}\right)$. Then noting that $1 - \lambda_+ = \lambda_-$ we can write$L(k+1) = A\left(\frac{1-\lambda_+^{k+1}}{\lambda_-}\right) + B\left(\frac{1-\lambda_-^{k+1}}{\lambda_+}\right) = \frac{A(\lambda_+ - \lambda_+^{k+2}) - B(\lambda_- - \lambda_-^{k+2})}{\lambda_t \lambda_-}$. Rearranging this and substituting in the constants A and B gives $L(k+1) = A\lambda_+^{K+2} + B\lambda_-^{k+2} - (A\lambda_+ B\lambda_-) = G_{k+2} - \frac{3(\lambda_- - \lambda_+)}{\lambda_- - \lambda_+} = G_{K+2} - 3$.

Question 6

(i) [2 marks] There are many possible diagrams that can be drawn here. A correct example is the following.

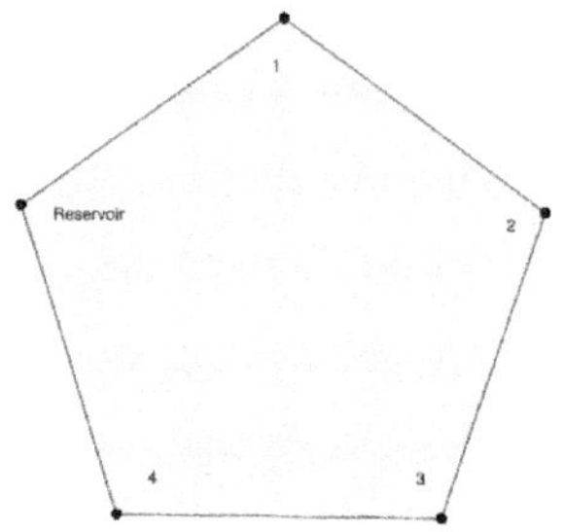

(ii) [3 marks] The minimum number of pipes used is $n+1$. To minimise the number of pipes, we want to visit each house exactly once, and so the diagram above shows a minimally connected network. This can be verified by removing one pipe, which leaves the whole system disconnected.

(iii) [3 marks] Again, there are multiple correct answers. One correct example is given below.

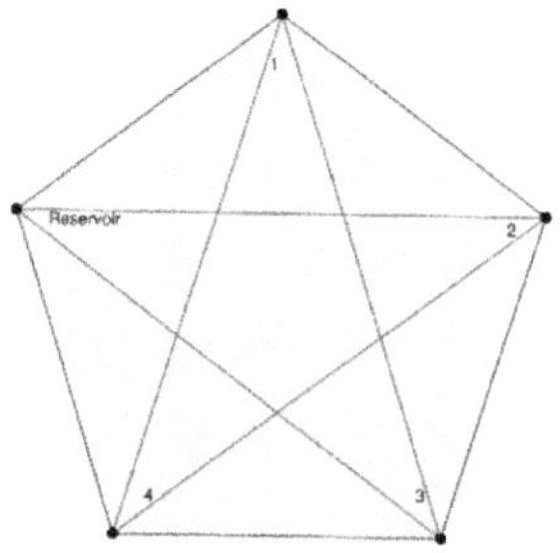

(iv) [6 marks] To avoid disconnecting the graph when one pipe is taken out, each house must have at least 3 pipes joining it. We minimise the number of pipes by introducing one source house in the middle, to which all the other houses are connected. Suppose we have n houses. Then there are $n + 1$ points on our graph when we include the reservoir. We introduce one source point, leaving n points on the outer edge of the graph. We connect these n points in the same way as part (ii) using n pipes. We then connect each of the n points on the outside to the source house placed in the middle, using another n pipes. This uses $n + n = 2n$ pipes in total. An example of this method can be seen in the figure below for $n = 5$. This is minimally connected because if we remove the source point and any other point, the graph ceases to be connected.

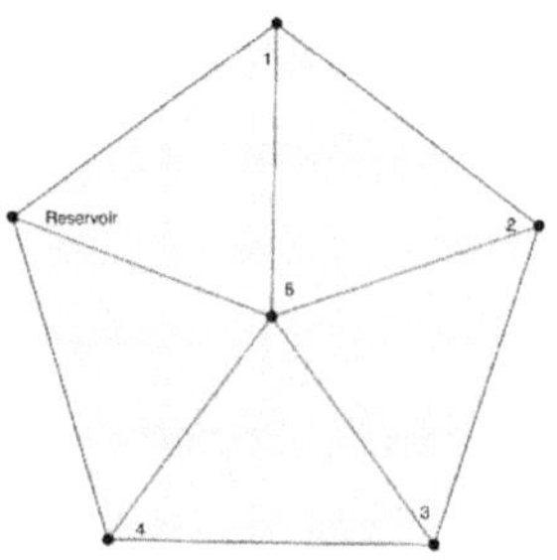

(v) [1 mark] From our minimally connected graph above, the total water quality is 3(n − 1) + n = 4n − 3 which is not necessarily a multiple of 3. A counterexample can be seen in the figure above.

Question 7

(i) [2 marks] Consider starting with the word M . Then applying the rule once gives the word MW. Applying the rule again gives the word $MWWM$. Finally applying the rule once more gives $MWWMWMMW$. This describes all words up to length 8.

(ii) [3 marks] Any word has length 2^k. When $k = 2n$, we are looking at the even steps in creating words. For a word to be palindromic, it has to be symmetric about its centre. Suppose we start with a symmetric word x. Then $y = xx^{-1}$ is an antisymmetric word. But applying the rule again gives $z = yy^{-1} = xx^{-1}x^{-1}x$ which turns an antisymmetric word y back into a symmetric one. M is trivially symmetric, and so every second step, i.e. the even-numbered ones, are palindromic words.

(iii) [3 marks] The rotation operation is the same as reversing the order of the word and then taking the inverse. Since words of length 2^{2n+1} are antisymmetric, then flipping it backwards is the same as swapping the first and second half of the word. In other words, that is writing $y = xx^{-1}$ as $x^{-1}x$ and taking the inverse of this so $y = x^{x-1}$ and therefore it remains invariant under the rotation operation.

(iv) [3 marks] As words of length 2^{2n} are palindromic, they are the same backwards as they are forwards. That is changing $y = x^{x-1}$ to $x^{-1}x$ does nothing. Then we have to take the inverse, and so we are left with $y^{-1} = x^{-1}x$. Therefore, the rotation operation is the same as the inversion operation for words of length 2^{2n}.

(v) [4 marks] Note that rule 2 does not have any effect on three of the same letter appearing in a row. However, rule I prohibits three of the same letter appearing in a row. This is because we start with M, and this produces the building block MW using the first rule. Longer words can only ever be built using MW or WM and so we cannot have three of the same letter in a row.

For three of the same letter, we must introduce a building block such as MM or WW. We could do this with a rule such as: 'if x is a word and y is a word, then xy is a word'. Note this will trivially produce the word MM then MMM.

PRACTICE PAPER 4

Question 1

A

[4 marks]

The answer is b.

$y = 3^{3r+3s-2r-5} \times 5^r = 3^{r-2s} \times 5^r \times 2^{2s-r}$. Thus we need $r - 2s \geq 0, 2s - r \geq 0, r \geq 0$. Therefore $r \geq 0$ and $r = 2s$.

B

[4 marks]

The answer is d.

The desired transformation is:

1. A translation of x_1 in the negative direction, giving an equation $y = f(x + x_1)$.
2. Reaction in the x axis, giving $y = -f(x + x_1)$.
3. A translation of $f(x_1)$ in the positive y direction, giving an equation $\eta = f(x_1) - f(x + x_1)$.

C

[4 marks]

The answer is a.

Suppose that $x^3 + ax^2 + bx + c$ has three consecutive integer roots. Then $x^3 + ax^2 + bx + c = (x - k)\big(x - (k+1)\big)(x - (k+2)) = x^3 - 3(k+1)x^2 + [k(k+2) + 2(k+1)^2]x - k(k+1)(k+2)$ for some integer k . Note that $\frac{c}{a} = \frac{k(k+2)}{3}$ and that $\frac{a}{3} = k + 1$ So the relation that must stand is $b = \frac{3c}{a} + \frac{4a^2}{9}$.

D

[4 marks]

The answer is d.

The graph of $sin\ x$ is a twofold stretch of $sin(2x)$. One needs to roughly divide the x axis into six equal regions, as the unit circle is divided, to see that $sin(2x) \geq sin\ x$ in the first, fourth and fifth regions.

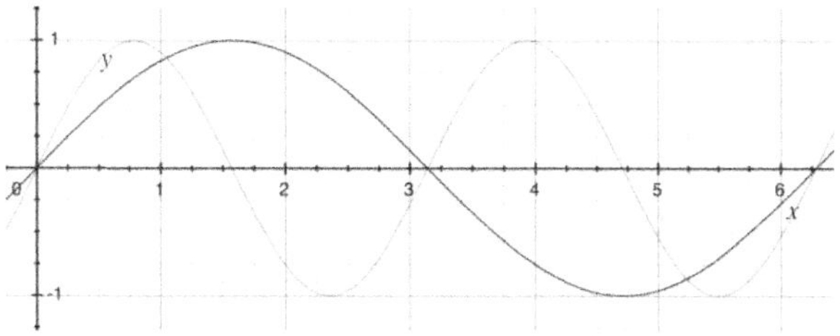

E

[4 marks]

The answer is c.

The graph of $y = \sin^2 x$ (shown in the first diagram below) will follow the same shape as $y = \sin(x)$ but with the negative sections reflected in the x axis. The graph of $y = x \sin^2 x$ (shown in the second diagram below) will stretch this as the magnitude of x grows and reflect the section with negative x values. Consider what happens when the outputs of the graph are the inputs into a log function. Inputs into a log function must be positive, and so the y values of $y = x \sin^2 x$ must be positive, which occurs when x is positive. Therefore, the answer must be a, b or c. $y = x \sin^2 x$ has y values greater than 1 and so $y = \log(x \sin^2 x)$ will have some positive values. Therefore, the answer is a or c. Now consider the first three peaks of the graph. Let X, Y, Z denote the x values of the peaks with $X \approx 2, Y \approx 5$ and $Z \approx 8$. It follows that $X \sin^2 X < Y \sin^2 Y < Z \sin^2 Z$ Therefore, since $log\ x$ is an increasing function for all x, $\log(X \sin^2 X) < \log(Y \sin^2 Y) < \log(Z \sin^2 Z)$. Only diagram c has the same corresponding three increasing peaks.

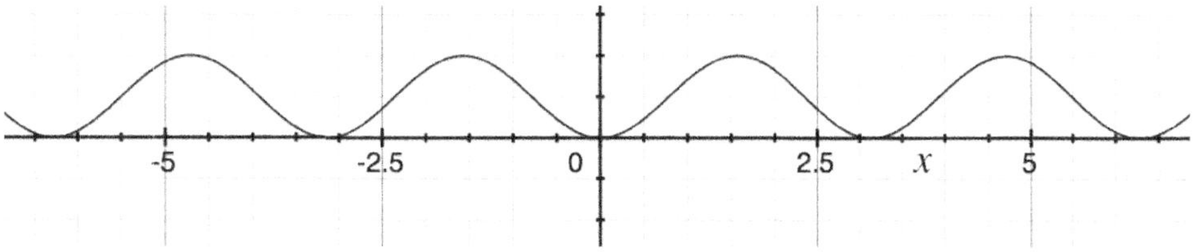

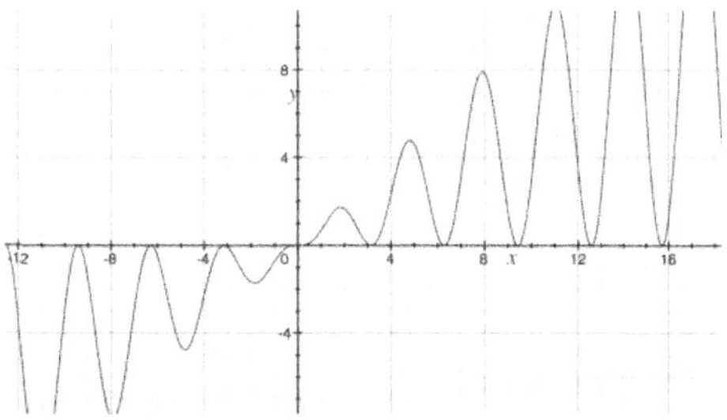

F

[4 marks]

The answer is e.

$\frac{1}{x} - x = \tan A$ rearranges to $x^2 + x\tan A - 1 = 0$, the discriminant of which is equal to $4\tan^2 A + 4 = 4(\tan^2 + 1) = \frac{(4\sin^2 A + \cos^2 A)}{\cos^2 A} = \frac{4}{\cos^2 A}$ which is always greater than or equal to zero. Therefore, the quadratic has a solution for all values of A.

G

[4 marks]

The answer is a.

For these 6 students, the probability of the award is $p = \frac{1}{2^n}$. Each student can either get the award with probability p or not get the award with probability $1 - p$, independent of all the other student's performances. This is a binomial probability and so the answer is ${}^6C_2 \times \left(\frac{1}{2^n}\right)^2 \times \left(1 - \frac{1}{2^n}\right)^4 = 15 \times \frac{(2^n-1)^4}{2^6 n}$.

H

[4 marks]

The answer is b.

We can write $\frac{1}{\cos x+2} - \frac{1}{\cos x+3} = \frac{1}{(\cos x+2)(\cos x+3)} = \frac{1}{\left(\cos x+\frac{5}{2}\right)^2 - \frac{1}{4}}$. Thus we must minimise $\cos x + \frac{5}{2}$. This has minimum value $-1 + \frac{5}{2} = \frac{3}{2}$ when $\cos x = -1$. Therefore, the maximum value is $\frac{1}{2}$.

I

[4 marks]

The answer is e.

We know that $f(x) = f(4 - x)$ and so $f(2 - x) = f\big(4 - (2 + x)\big) = f(2 + x)$ and so $f(x)$ is symmetric in the line $x = 2$. Therefore $y = f(x)$ must be c, d or e. Now if $\frac{1}{f(x)} = 0$ at $x = 0$, then f rows very quickly as x becomes small. This rules out c. Finally, $f(-x) = -f(x)$ and so the bottom left quadrant is a reflection in the x axis of the upper right quadrant.

J

[4 marks]

The answer is a.

The area in property 1 is $\int_n^{n+1} ax^2 + bx + 1dx = \frac{a}{3}(n+1)^3 + \frac{b}{2}(n+1)^2 + (n+1) - \frac{a}{3}n^3 - \frac{b}{2}n^2 - n = an^2 + (a+b)n + \left(\frac{a}{3} + \frac{b}{2} + 1\right)$. Therefore, we must have $an^2 + (a+b)n + \left(\frac{a}{3} + \frac{b}{2} + 1\right) > 1$ for all n. Substituting in $n = 0$ gives $a > \frac{-3b}{2}$.

Question 2

(i) [2 marks] $f(-x) = (-x)^2 = x^2 = f(x)$ and $g(-x) = (-x)^3 = -x^3 = -9(x)$.

(ii) [2 marks] No. A correct counterexample is, for example, $f(x) = 1 + x$ with $f(-x) = 1 - x$ which is neither equal to $f(x)$ nor $-f(x)$ for all x.

(iii) [2 marks] If f is both even and odd, then for all $x, f(-x) = f(x)$ and $-f(-x) = f(x)$. Adding these together gives $f(x) = 0$ for all x. Thus the only such function is the function that is zero everywhere.

(iv) [3 marks]

$g(-x) = f(g(-x))(-g(x)) = f(-g(x)) = f(9(x)) = fg(x)$ for all x.

$gf(-x) = g(f(-x)) = g(f(x)) = gf(x)$ for all x.

$f^2(-x) = f(f(-x)) = f(f(x)) = f^2(x)$ for all x.

(v) [3 marks] $f(x) + g(x) = \frac{h(x)+h(-x)}{2} + \frac{h(x)-h(-x)}{2} = h(x)$. Furthermore, $f(-x) = \frac{h(-x)+h(x)}{2}$ so f is even. Similarly, we can write $g(-x) = \frac{h(-x)-h(x)}{2} = -g(x)$ so g is odd. Given any function h we can always construct this f and g. Therefore, every function can be written as the sum of an odd function and an even function.

(vi) [3 marks] Assume that h can be written in two ways, as the sum of an even and odd function i.e. $h(x) = f_1(x) + g_1(x) = f_2(x) + g_2(x)$ where $f_i(x)$ are even functions and g_i are odd functions. This means that $f_1(x) - f_2(x) = g_2(x) - g_1(x)$. Note that the left side of the equation is an even function, and the right side is an odd function. So these must be equal to 0, from part (iii). This implies that $f_1 = f_2 = f$ and $g_1 = g_2 = g$. So $h(x) = f(x) + g(x)$ is the unique decomposition in this way.

Question 3

(i) [3 marks]

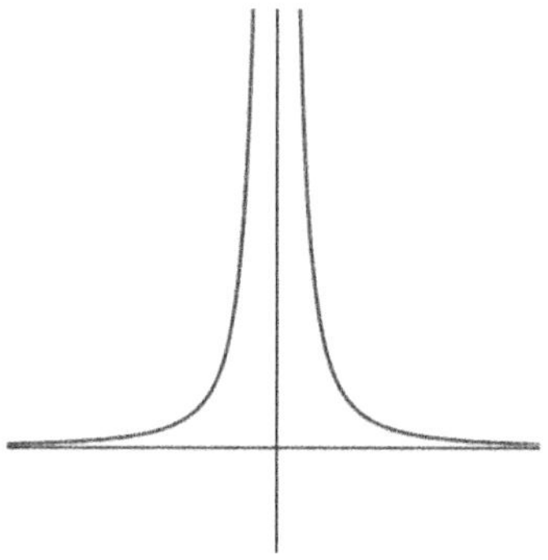

$$\int_1^N \frac{1}{x^2}\,dx = \left[-\frac{1}{x}\right]_1^N = 1 - \frac{1}{N}$$

(ii) [1 mark] This integral approaches 1 as N becomes large because $lim_{N\to\infty}\frac{1}{N} = 0$.

(iii) [4 marks]

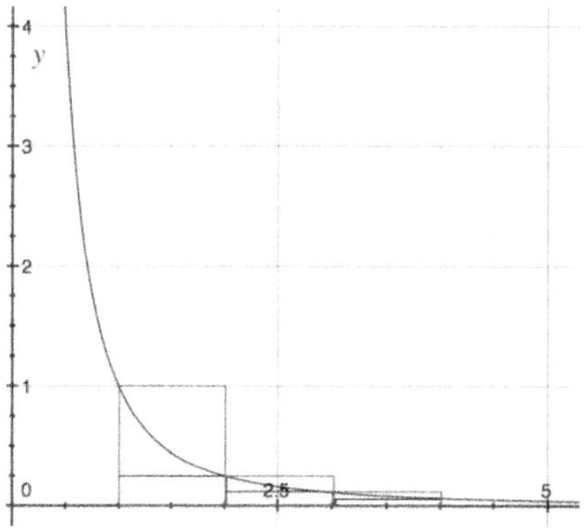

These bounds can be attained by using a series of rectangles with their top left or top right corner on the graph of $y = \frac{1}{x^2}$ (these correspond to over-estimations or underestimations of the integral, respectively).

From the diagram we obtain $\int_1^n \frac{1}{x^2}dx < 1 + \cdots + \frac{1}{(n-1)^2}$ and $\int_1^n \frac{1}{x^2}dx > \frac{1}{2^2} + \cdots + \frac{1}{n^2}$. Thus we must have $\int_1^n \frac{1}{x^2}dx + \frac{1}{n^2} < 1 + \frac{1}{2^2} + \cdots + \frac{1}{(n-1)^2} < 1 + \int_1^N \frac{1}{x^2}dx.$

Substituting in the value of the integral, we get $1 - \frac{1}{n} + \frac{1}{n^2} < 1 + \frac{1}{2^2} + \cdots + \frac{1}{(n-1)^2} + \frac{1}{n^2} < 1 + 1 - \frac{1}{n}.$

(iv) [2 marks] Finally, letting $n \to \infty$, we are left with $1 < \sum_{k=1}^{\infty}\frac{1}{k^2} < 2.$

(v) [5 marks] Here we would like to employ the same technique as above. So we wish to find the function that, when taking rectangular strips of width 1, gives an area that looks like $\sqrt{k}$. The obvious choice is $y = \sqrt{x}$.

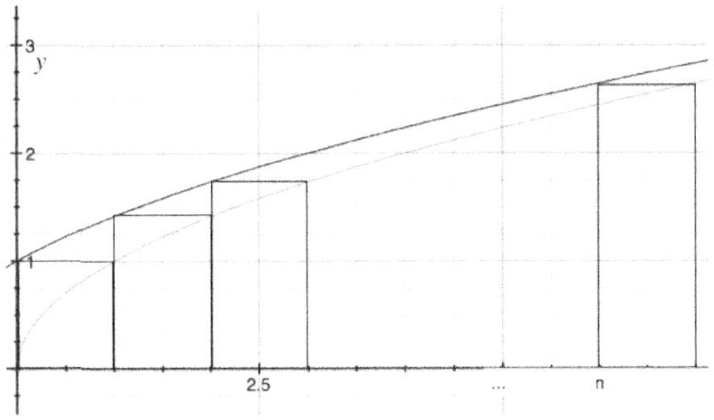

If we are looking for an overestimate, then the right-hand corner of each box touches the graph. An underestimate occurs if we draw rectangles such that the left-hand corner of each rectangle touches the curve. The rectangles are sandwiched between $y = \sqrt{x}$ and $y = \sqrt{x+1}$. We see that an underestimate for $y = \sqrt{x+1}$ in this manner still gives an overestimate for $y = \sqrt{x}$.

Therefore $\int_0^{n+1} \sqrt{x}\, dx < 1 + \cdots + \sqrt{n} < \int_0^{n+1} \sqrt{x+1}\, dx$. Evaluating the integral, we are left with $\frac{2(n+1)^{\frac{3}{2}}}{3} < 1 + \cdots + \sqrt{n} < \frac{2(n+2)^{\frac{3}{2}}}{3} - \frac{2}{3}$.

Setting $n = 80$ and substituting into the previous equation gives $\frac{2}{3} \times 9^3 < 1 + \cdots + \sqrt{80} < \frac{2}{3} \times \left(\left(\sqrt{82}\right)^3 - 1 \right)$ which reduces to $486 < 1 + \cdots + \sqrt{80} < 550$.

We note that to get this last bound we can use

$$\frac{2}{3} \times \left(\left(\sqrt{82}\right)^3 - 1 \right) = \frac{2}{3} \times \left(82\sqrt{82} - 1\right) < \frac{2}{3} \times \left(82\sqrt{100} - 1\right) = \frac{2}{3} \times (819) = 546 < 500$$

Question 4

(i) [1 mark] $c = \mu b + \lambda a$

(ii) [3 marks] Considering the shared side, $\mu a = \lambda b$. Thus $\mu\left(\frac{a^2}{b} + b\right) = c$ so $\mu = \frac{bc}{a^2+b^2}$ and $\lambda = \frac{ac}{a^2+b^2}$.

(iii) [3marks] The angles opposite the diameter form a 90 degree angle. Therefore, the two smaller triangles form a right-angle triangle. By Pythagoras: $(\mu c)^2 + (\lambda c)^2 = c^2$. Thus $\mu^2 + \lambda^2 = 1$.

(iv) [3marks] The area of the three triangles is given by $A_1 = \frac{1}{2}(1 + \mu^2 + \lambda^2)ab = \frac{1}{2} \times 2 \times ab = ab$. The area of the circle is given by $A_2 = \pi r^2 = \pi \times \left(\frac{c}{2}\right)^2 = \frac{\pi c^2}{4}$. Therefore, the proportion of the area of the circle taken up by the three triangles is $\frac{A_1}{A_2} = \frac{4ab}{\pi c^2}$.

(v) [2 marks] In the limit as $a \to b$, $\frac{A_1}{A_2} \to \frac{4a^2}{11c}$ and noting by Pythagoras that $2a^2 = c^2$, we must have $\frac{A_1}{A_2} \to \frac{2}{\pi}$. Note that in this case, the three triangles form a square.

(vi) [3 marks] The circle is inscribed within a square as $a \to b$. Without loss of generality, set $a = 1$.Then as $a \to b$, $C \to \sqrt{2}$ by Pythagoras. The area of the big circle is given by $A_3 = \pi r^2 = \pi \times \left(\frac{\sqrt{2}}{2}\right)^2 = \frac{\pi}{2}$. The radius of the small circle is $\frac{a}{2} = \frac{1}{2}$ since we have set $a = 1$. Therefore, the area of the small circle is $A_4 = \pi \times \left(\frac{1}{2}\right)^2 = \frac{\pi}{4}$. Therefore, the proportion of the small circle to the big circle is given by $\frac{A_4}{A_3} = \frac{1}{2}$.

Question 5

(i) [3 marks] Suppose we start with a right turn. Then the next move must be a left, as we are looking at $(4{,}1)$ routes, which is impossible. Therefore, we must start with a double left turn. It then remains to choose the order in which to take two more left turns and a right turn. The options are RLL, LRL or LLR. It is impossible to complete RLL since this would take you off the grid. The following tree diagrams for LRL and LLR show that the only $(4;\ 1)$ route ending in the bottom right corner is.

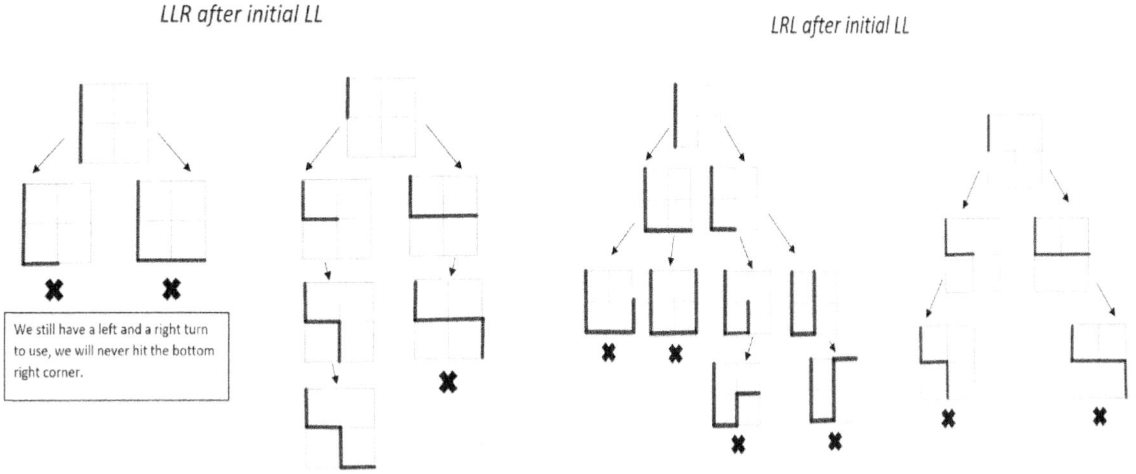

(ii) [4 marks] In the previous part, we established that a route with only one right turn must start with a double left turn. This doesn't take you to the bottom right corner without adding in some more turns. Therefore, we must have $n > 2$. There is a total of 12 individual line segments in the grid, none of which can be revisited in a route, so we must also have $n \leq 12$. To see that $n \neq 12$, consider the top left horizontal line segment. It cannot be traversed left to right because the route must start with a double left turn. Therefore, you cannot start at the top left corner without re-traversing a line segment. It cannot be traversed right to left because this would create a loop. Therefore at least one of these 12 line segments cannot be traversed, so $2 < n < 12$.

(iii) [4 marks] A series of right and left turns has the same effect on the direction faced irrespective of their order. You start facing North and take exactly one right turn, after which you will face East. To arrive at the bottom right square, you will finish facing either East or South. Therefore the n left turns create either a 360 full turn or a $\frac{3}{4} \times 360$ full turn. n must be a multiple of 4 to create a full turn so n is either a multiple of 4 or one less than a multiple of 4.

(iv) [4 marks] The route must start with the top-left vertical line segment, and end with the bottom right horizontal line segment (since 8 is a multiple of 4 - see previous part of question). If you continue South, you will have to turn left and complete the route (a large L shape) which doesn't have enough turns. If you instead turn left, there are two options:

1. If you turn left again you will be forced to take 2 right turns
2. If you keep heading East, there is no way to approach the bottom right square facing East.

So this route cannot occur.

Question 6

(i) [1 mark] $3 = 2^2 - 1,\ 5 = 3^2 - 2^2,\ 7 = 4^2 - 3^2$

(ii) [4 marks] The algorithm can be given by the following steps:

1. Let x be an odd number
2. Subtract 1 from x
3. Half the result
4. Call the resulting number n
5. Write $x = (n+1)^2 - n^2$

Proof: $\left(1 + \frac{(x-1)}{2}\right)^2 - \left(\frac{x-1}{2}\right)^2 = \frac{(x+1)^2-(x-1)^2}{4} = x$. The algorithm produces an integer for all odd inputs. Therefore, all odd numbers can be written in the form $(n+1)^2 - n^2$.

(iii) [3 marks] Suppose that $x = (n+1)^4 - n^4$ for some integer n. Then $x = ((n+1)^2 + n^2)((n+1)^2 - n^2)$. Let $a = (n+1)^2 + n^2$ and $b = (n+1)^2 - n^2$. Then $x = ab$ and $a + b = 2(n+1)^2$.

(iv) [3 marks] $175 = 1 \times 175 = 5 \times 35 = 7 \times 25$

$1 + 175 = 176,\ 5 + 35 = 40,\ 7 + 25 = 32$

$\frac{176}{2} = 88,\ \frac{40}{2} = 20,\ \frac{32}{2} = 16$, the last of which is a square number. Let $16 = (n+1)^2$, so $n = 3$. Then $4^4 - 3^4 = (4^2 + 3^2)(4^2 - 3^2) = 25 \times 7 = 175$.

(v) [4 marks]

1. Call the input number x
2. Find all pairs of integers (a, b) such that $ab = x$
3. For each pair calculate $\frac{a+b}{2}$
4. If none of the resulting numbers are square numbers, then x cannot be written in the form $(n+1)^4 - n^4$
5. If one of these numbers is a square number, take its square root and subtract one.
6. Call this output number n
7. $x = (n+1)^4 - n^4$

Question 7

(i) [2 marks] There are 3 sentences of length 2 starting with Zap: $ZapZoop$, $ZapZap$, $ZapZeep$. The 7 sentences of length 3 start with Zap and are given by $ZapZapZap$, $ZapZapZoop$, $ZapZapZeep$, $ZapZoopZoop$, $ZapZoopZap$, $ZapZeepZeep$, $ZapZeepZap$

(ii) [4 marks] Every sentence starting with a $'Zoop'$ can be turned into a sequence starting with Zeep by changing all the $Zoops$ to $Zeeps$ and vice versa. Likewise, all Zeep-sentences can be turned into Zoop-sentences. So there are equal numbers of each type, with length n. Starting with a Zoop, then the next letter must be a $Zoop$ or a Zap. Therefore, any sequence of length n which starts with a $Zoop$ is a $Zoop$ followed by a valid sequence of length $n-1$ starting with a $Zoop$ or a Zap. That is, $o(n) = o(n-1) + a(n-1)$. Starting with a Zap, then the next letter can be a $Zoop$, Zap or $Zeep$. Thus $a(n) = o(n-1) + a(n1-) + e(n-1) = 2o(n-1) + a(n-1)$ since $e(k) = o(k)$ for all k. Rearranging gives the required result.

(iii) [4 marks] A sequence of length n must start with one of $Zoop$, Zap or $Zeep$. Therefore $z(n) = o(n) + a(n) + e(n) = 2o(n) + a(n)$. Using this and the above relations gives: $z(3) = 2o(3) + a(3) = 2\big(o(2) + a(2)\big) + a(3) = 2(2+3) + 7 = 17$ and $z(4) = 2o(4) + a(4) = 2\big(o(3) + (3)\big) + 2o(3) + a(3) = 4o(3) + 21 = 4 \times 5 + 21 = 41$.

(iv) [5 marks] Consider first the case when the sentence is odd. If a sentence is friendly, then when it is reversed, the middle word stays in the same position and so must remain unchanged by the $Zoop - Zap$ swap. Therefore, it must be a Zap.

Now consider when the sentence is even. To make an even length friendly sentence, we start by taking any sentence that starts with a Zap. We reverse a sentence by swapping $Zoops$ for $Zeeps$ and vice versa. We then place the new reversed sentence and put it in front of the original. This will leave us with two $Zaps$ in the middle of the sentence. Note that all even length friendly sentences can be made this way, because there can't be adjacent $ZoopZeeps$ in the middle. We can make an odd length sentence in the same way but dropping one of the middle Zaps. This gives $f(n) = a\left(\frac{n+1}{2}\right)$ if n is odd, and $f(n) = a\left(\frac{n}{2}\right)$ if n is even. Thus $f(2k) - f^{(2k-1)} = a(k) - a(k) = 0$.

FINAL ADVICE

Arrive well-rested, well-fed and well hydrated

The MAT is an intensive test, so make sure you're ready for it. Ensure you get a good night's sleep before the exam (there is little point cramming) and don't miss breakfast. If you're taking water into the exam then make sure you've been to the toilet before so you don't have to leave during the exam. Make sure you're well-rested and fed in order to be at your best!

Move on

If you're struggling, move on. Every question has equal weighting and there is no negative marking. All of the questions in the MAT are intended to be challenging, so don't' be demoralised by moving on partway through a question. You may find the change of focus helps you think of new ways to approach the problem and remember that you'll be getting credit for your working, even if it doesn't lead you to the final answer.

Afterword

Remember that the route to a high score is your approach and practice. Don't fall into the trap that "*you can't prepare for the MAT*"– this could not be further from the truth. With knowledge of the test, some useful time-saving techniques and plenty of practice you can dramatically boost your score.

Work hard, never give up and do yourself justice.

Good luck!

What's Next?

- ✓ Three books crammed into one!
- ✓ Includes complete Course profiles and College insights from Oxbridge admissions tutors and current students
- ✓ 100+ of examples of real personal statements written by Oxbridge Applicants
- ✓ Each statement analysed with feedback
- ✓ Covers every major subject at Oxford & Cambridge
- ✓ Work experience advice- how to arrange it and how to stand out from the crowd

- ✓ 200+ Real Oxbridge interview Questions
- ✓ Covers Engineering, Natural Sciences, Chemistry, Material Sciences, Physics, Maths, Computer Sciences, Earth Sciences interview questions at Oxford and Cambridge
- ✓ Includes model answers for every question with commentary from Admissions Tutors
- ✓ Written by Cambridge & Oxford Science Tutors & Professors

ABOUT US

We currently publish over 85 titles across a range of subject areas – covering specialised admissions tests, examination techniques, personal statement guides, plus everything else you need to improve your chances of getting on to competitive courses such as medicine and law, as well as into universities such as Oxford and Cambridge.

Outside of publishing we also operate a highly successful tuition division called UniAdmissions. This company was founded in 2013 by Dr Rohan Agarwal and Dr David Salt, both Cambridge Medical graduates with several years of tutoring experience. Since then, every year, hundreds of applicants and schools work with us on our programmes. Through the programmes we offer, we deliver expert tuition, exclusive course places, online courses, best-selling textbooks and much more.

With a team of over 1,000 Oxbridge tutors and a proven track record, UniAdmissions have quickly become the UK's number one admissions company.

Visit and engage with us at:

Website (UniAdmissions): www.uniadmissions.co.uk

Facebook: www.facebook.com/uniadmissionsuk

YOUR FREE BOOK

Thanks for purchasing this Ultimate Book. Readers like you have the power to make or break a book – hopefully you found this one useful and informative. *UniAdmissions* would love to hear about your experiences with this book. As thanks for your time we'll send you another ebook from our Ultimate Guide series absolutely FREE!

How to Redeem Your Free Ebook

1) Find the book you have on your Amazon

purchase history or your email receipt to help find the book on Amazon.

2) On the product page at the Customer Reviews area, click 'Write a customer review'. Write your review and post it! Copy the review page or take a screen shot of the review you have left.

3) Head over to www.uniadmissions.co.uk/free-book and select your chosen free ebook!

Your ebook will then be emailed to you – it's as simple as that!

Alternatively, you can buy all the titles at

www.uniadmissions.co.uk

Printed in Great Britain
by Amazon

45427987R00051